Integrity®
From Marvin
Windows and Doors

MW00680669

AN EASY ANSWER
that comes in a tough package.

Marvin Windows and Doors is known for its custom capabilities. So it's no surprise that our line of standard-sized Integrity products would offer some exceptional benefits.

Piece-of-cake installation that means no call backs later.

Beautiful solid wood paired with Ultrex®, an exterior so advanced it's virtually indestructible.

The more you get to know Integrity, the more you'll realize that there are many differences that will make it your new standard. Take a look.

And discover what we're made of.

Built to perform.

If you made your own windows, this is how you'd do it.

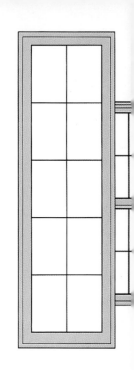

In the early days of homebuilding,

the person who poured the foundation was the person who raised the frame, who built the roof, who made and installed the windows and doors. Quality control wasn't an issue, because the house was being painstakingly built by the person who was going to live in it. Anything less would just mean more work later.

Today, your home is built with a small army, using tools and materials from places you've never been, made by people that you hope are qualified and dedicated. You have no option but to place your trust in the hands of these strangers, since making your own bricks or shingles isn't really possible.

Easy-to-order windows and doors you can count on, in the most popular sizes.

Installation shortcuts, like an exceptional exterior finish, pre-installed screens, pre-attached nailing fins and pre-assembled bows, bays and patio doors. Delivered in perfect shape, stretch-wrapped and square so they are ready to go at the job site.

With all this in mind, and in the tradition of places constructed as sturdy and strong as the name we present

Integrity
From Marvin®
Windows and Doors

Windows and doors made of a unique combination of state-of-the-art and classic materials. Weather-tight. Solid. Beautiful wood interiors. Designed to last for generations, backed by a ten-year warranty. Created by the people at Marvin Windows and Doors, a name synonymous with reliability, tradition and excellence, and above all else, Integrity windows and doors are *Built to perform.*

The ULTREX® difference.

One of the most remarkable things about Ultrex is what it doesn't do. Cold and heat cause minimal expansion or contraction; considerably less than you'd find in other window materials. In addition, Ultrex is remarkably non-conductive, insulating extreme weather temperatures from the glass in our windows and doors as well as from the interior of the home itself. And it's so low-maintenance, you don't have to think about anything but the view.

NFRC ratings.

We have a history of setting high standards. In fact, Marvin is a founding member of the National Fenestration Rating Council, a non-profit trade organization that defined an energy performance rating system for the entire window and door industry. Different factors are considered, including light transmission as well as heat loss and gain under different conditions. Of course, we made sure that Integrity® was worthy of one of the highest performance ratings available. So in the end, you can be sure that you're comparing apples to apples. And that you're not stuck with a lemon.

Low E II and argon gas.

Low E II glazings are a simple means of minimizing summer heat gain and reducing heat loss in the winter. Think of them as microscopic shutters that allow warming low-angle winter sun into a home while filtering high-angle summer light. At the same time, UV rays are screened to reduce fading and damage to upholstery and carpets. Argon gas and a warm edge spacer are also part of one of the most effective glazings in the industry, which we're offering as a standard feature. It all adds up to long-term savings for you, making Integrity penny-wise in the beginning, pound-wise to the end.

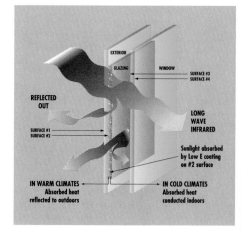

Low E II

ENERGY EFFICIENCY

A performance you'll applaud for years to come.

Integrity assembly above available as a field mull only.

The cost of a home isn't just the bottom line on a mortgage. Heating and cooling costs continue to be an important issue with homeowners. We build Integrity® products with this in mind, providing windows and doors that aren't just an excellent value in home construction. They're an investment in the future of a home.

Ask About ENERGY STAR

Integrity
From Marvin ®
Windows and Doors
Built to perform.

This product is qualified as ENERGY STAR for the regions indicated below: Regions 1, 2 and 3.

■ **Region 1**
Mostly Heating

■ **Region 2**
Heating and Cooling

■ **Region 3**
Mostly Cooling

ENERGY STAR® approved.

From refrigerators to computer monitors, fans to windows and doors, the ENERGY STAR rating is only granted to products that reduce energy use. The U.S. Department of Energy and the U.S. Environmental Protection Agency created this program to help people make smart, long-term choices for their new or remodeled home. Since Integrity windows and doors are twice as efficient as an average window produced ten years ago, they not only meet the standards necessary to qualify for the ENERGY STAR rating – they exceed it.

standard
features

Right from the start.

There's nothing everyday about our standard window or door. That's because we begin beyond what many people consider top of the line. Every interior is all wood, nothing less. State-of-the-art engineering ensures solid, secure opening and closing. Attention to even the smallest design details is mandatory, such as handles that match the contour of your hand and a traditional millwork look in our aluminum cladding.

From there, the options are up to you. Depending on the type of home you're building, and where it's located, and how true to your vision you want to be. Choose the right type of glass for your region, so you can invite or deflect the sun's warmth. Add aluminum cladding, and enjoy a virtually maintenance-free exterior. Put a new twist on a traditional grille pattern. Create a wall of light, or focus on a single stunning view. All easily possible. Every single one *Made for You.*

Is your imagination up to the challenge?

The soaring Gothic arches of a European cathedral. The front window in the bank of your home town. The quirky dormer in your grandmother's attic — that funny little window you swore you'd have in your own house someday. Anything. Everything. If it inspires you, chances are, we can build it.

You can design a signature lite pattern that carries through all the windows in your home. Or use an oversized — or particularly small — opening to make a statement. For that really large project, custom color capabilities can match your exterior cladding to almost anything, even the begonias that line the driveway. And the real beauty is that anything we create for you will offer nearly the same energy efficiency and *Made for You* flexibility as the rest of our line. No matter how we're pushing the limits with a custom window or door, we refuse to compromise on performance or reliability. Because before a window or door is a work of art, it has to be a Marvin.

MARVIN
Windows and Doors
Made for you.®

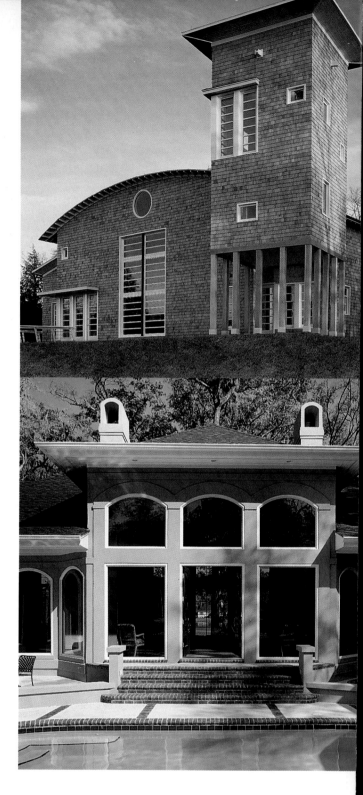

custom
possibilities

A STUDY OF HOME™

bringing the outside in & the inside out

Editor	Bruce Arant
Plans Editor	Tina Libe
Graphic Designers	Heather Guthrie
	Jeff Dedlow
	Beverly Nelligan
	Annette Guy
Rendering Colorization	Tammi Camilen
	Alva Louden
Rendering Illustrators	Silvia Boyd
	Shawn Doherty
	Paul Gernandt
	George McDonald, dec.
	Gerald Metzger
Technical Advisers	Tom Clark
	Carl Cuozzo
	Rob Phillips
Writer	Joyce Brown
Circulation Manager	Priscilla Ivey
Co-Publishers	Dennis Brozak
	Linda Reimer

A STUDY OF HOME™
~ bringing the outside in & the inside out

IS PUBLISHED BY:

Design Basics Publications
11112 John Galt Blvd., Omaha, NE 68137
web – www.designbasics.com
e-mail – info@designbasics.com

Chief Executive Officer	Dennis Brozak
President	Linda Reimer
Director of Marketing	Kevin Blair
Business Development	Paul Foresman
Controller	Janie Murnane
Editor-in-Chief	Bruce Arant

Cover Photo: plan 2285 Prairie

Builder: Sudon Brothers Inc.

library of congress
control number: 2001093620

ISBN: 1-892150-24-7

One Story

PLAN #	PLAN NAME	SQ. FT.	PAGE #
6740	balentine	1142	44
24045	glenco	1263	14
1551	logan	1271	45
6750	aiken	1311	45
3102	aspen	1339	25
24048	cartwright	1359	65
8091	winter woods	1360	58
8013	gabriel bay	1392	65
24126	bellglade	1407	57
24051	cabrie	1541	80
2537	tahoe	1580	18
1767	rosebury	1604	46
5179	spenlow	1650	47
5001	anson	1653	71
8016	jennys brook	1691	54
8505	eden	1724	59
8527	la crosse	1724	38
9187	creekbend manor	1751	81
24003	tuxford	1762	59
24020	brooks	1819	33
9198	windrush estate	1876	83
8518	vanceboro	1902	15
1748	sinclair	1911	55
9201	waterside estate	1926	84
24021	barber	1980	51
1539	mansfield	1996	43
9171	westcott manor	2040	79
24038	clarkson	2126	48
24027	oakland	2144	78
8045	coopers farm	2151	49
9185	longworth estate	2211	77
9207	briar manor	2331	82
9191	crescent court	2393	41
2206	hawkesbury	2498	50
24153	wellborn	2512	85
5503	briarton	2586	39
9120	whitmore	3312	86

1 1/2 Story

PLAN #	PLAN NAME	SQ. FT.	PAGE #
3121	bellamy	1660	60
2245	tyndale	1685	29
8095	sun valley	1694	64
3089	parnell	1712	22
4133	marcell	1772	21
2281	ingram	1778	64
3385	brittany	1788	56
8037	carriage hills	1802	61
8084	brook valley	1865	56
1330	trenton	1869	42
9195	sherwood estates	1902	93
24154	stendal	1980	13
8507	smithport	2059	61

1 1/2 Story

PLAN #	PLAN NAME	SQ. FT.	PAGE #
2312	meredith	2113	43
5149	camrose	2190	42
8520	mindoro	2218	51
2057	bedford	2226	20
24138	whitfield	2252	70
1864	kensington	2278	30
24139	roseland	2349	76
1862	manchester	2353	54
24144	alanton	2382	74
24009	wainright	2420	46
8506	dobson	2425	62
24142	cottondale	2438	34
5519	fairmont	2448	75
2309	edmonton	2579	55
8519	ryland	2593	68
5520	philipsburg	2615	24
9174	stanton showcase	2638	88
9183	greatwood showcase	2665	91
24011	oliver	2688	62
9179	timber crest	2815	72
2476	dundee	2884	53
9162	tealwood estates	3072	69
9211	timberfield	3259	89
9214	balleroy	3335	90
24041	lagoda	3914	36
2016	churchill	3950	52

Two Story

PLAN #	PLAN NAME	SQ. FT.	PAGE #
6711	silverdale	1491	19
6715	sycamore	1495	57
2526	arbor	1605	47
24043	inverness	1632	17
6705	hopewell	1650	58
24044	farrelton	1823	44
8100	pebble creek	1844	63
1752	lancaster	1846	41
2235	albany	1931	49
9176	baldwin court	2042	92
8526	sarona	2061	32
8523	bridgeland	2084	40
8500	castalia	2200	60
1019	hazelton	2219	31
5518	kaitlyn	2279	28
8503	creedmoor	2324	63
8515	glendon	2354	27
1553	kendall	2387	48
9172	bibury manor	2438	67
8038	stone creek	2498	50
8510	wilkesboro	2638	53
3246	jennings	2644	37
2779	leawood	2689	52
3316	saratoga	3684	26

bringing the Outside In

Though we build our homes as a place of shelter from the elements of nature, it seems we do our best to stay close to the great outdoors — even while we're inside. This desire to bring the outdoors in has become more easily attained in recent years, due to advancements in the world of windows.

Over the last few decades, the number and styles of windows used in new home design has increased dramatically. It's easy to see why. Homes that are filled with natural light lift our spirits, open up rooms and make even smaller areas seem more spacious. Windows have become "see-through walls" connecting us to the natural world, broadening our perspective and helping us feel less closed in by our own cares.

On the exterior, unique windows are often used as focal points. The choice of windows defines a home's personality, whether charming or sophisticated. Windows also reveal a home's warmth — childrens' artwork displayed for passersby, the amber glow of a lamp streaming out

Photo Courtesy Of: Integrity® Windows and Doors

into the dark of night, a Christmas tree with multi-colored bulbs.

Inside and out, windows provide lovely views while bringing character and warmth to our homes.

In as much as we strive to bring the outdoors in, we also want our homes to extend the indoors out. The popularity of outdoor living spaces – porches, specifically – has no doubt been spurred by our longing for a simpler place and time. The very presence of a porch makes any home seem more inviting, and stirs something deep inside – something warm and comfortable.

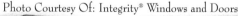
Photo Courtesy Of: Integrity® Windows and Doors

bringing the outside in . . .
Walls of windows flood our homes with natural light and provide everchanging murals to delight out senses. (above and left)

. . . and the inside out
Porches are places to lose our nearsightedness and expand our outlook… places to retreat from our daily hustle and bustle while reaching out to neighbors and guests. (opposite page)

& the Inside Out

Here, we look at the ways windows and glass doors bring the outdoors into our homes and how porches expand our living spaces to the outside.

In an impersonal world of automated answering, lengthy identification numbers and gigantic shopping malls, is it any wonder we yearn for the days of family-owned corner shops and neighbors stopping by to visit on the front porch?

A STUDY OF HOME™ ~ bringing the outside in & the inside out presents 100 light-filled home designs with big, beautiful windows and charming, relaxing porches. We hope you'll find the perfect design for a bright, cheery home – your own personal retreat, and a welcoming place to gather family and friends.

bringing the Outside In

This photo is shown for example purposes only and is not from the stendal.

Photo Courtesy Of:
Integrity® Windows and Doors

windows as focal points

Without a doubt, windows are one of the elements that draws the most attention to a home's exterior. On older homes, they were often grouped in twos and threes, multi-paned and generously trimmed. Queen Anne homes were noted for their combinations of bay, arched and round windows. Craftsman and Prairie styles often incorporated stained glass.

During the mass production of the 40s, 50s and 60s, economical casement, sliding and awning windows became the norm. Cape Cod homes usually included dormers and two-pane windows. Ranch and split-level houses featured a big, wide "picture" window in the living room and a set of patio doors in the dining area.

On today's new homes, windows are once again focal points – not only on the exterior, but on the inside as well. A great room fireplace may be flanked by tall windows topped with trapezoid transoms. Graceful Palladian windows frequently add an air of sophistication in master bedrooms and dining rooms. Large transoms create dramatic entries. Yet even a small, well-placed window can provide a strong statement.

www.designbasics.com

the stendal

#50C ~24154 price code 19

1467 main floor
513 second floor
1980 total sq. ft.
NOTE: 9 ft. main level walls

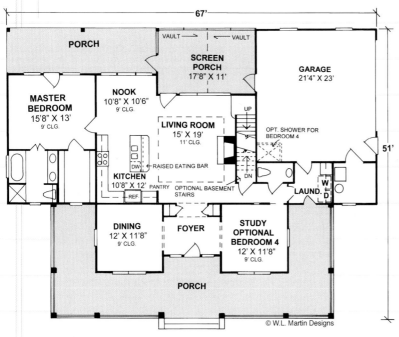

67'

PORCH

VAULT →   ← VAULT

SCREEN PORCH
17'8" X 11'

GARAGE
21'4" X 23'

MASTER BEDROOM
15'8" X 13'
9' CLG.

NOOK
10'8" X 10'6"
9' CLG.

LIVING ROOM
15' X 19'
11' CLG.

UP

OPT. SHOWER FOR BEDROOM 4

51'

RAISED EATING BAR

DW

KITCHEN
10'8" X 12'

REF.

PANTRY

DN

OPTIONAL BASEMENT STAIRS

LAUND.

W D

DINING
12' X 11'8"
9' CLG.

FOYER

STUDY OPTIONAL BEDROOM 4
12' X 11'8"
9' CLG.

PORCH

© W.L. Martin Designs

Stacked windows under a pair of gables add symmetry and harmony.

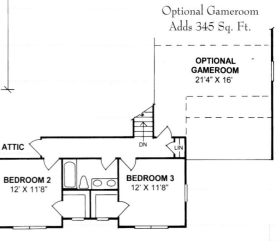

Optional Gameroom
Adds 345 Sq. Ft.

OPTIONAL GAMEROOM
21'4" X 16'

ATTIC

DN

LIN

BEDROOM 2
12' X 11'8"

BEDROOM 3
12' X 11'8"

design basics inc
HOME PLAN DESIGN SERVICE

the glenco

#50C ~24045   price code 12

1263 total sq. ft.

NOTE: 9 ft. main level walls

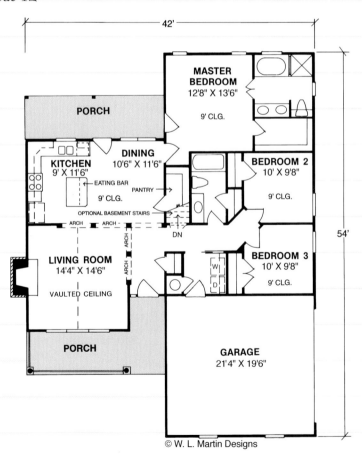

MASTER
BEDROOM
12'8" X 13'6"

9' CLG.

PORCH

DINING
10'6" X 11'6"

KITCHEN
9' X 11'6"

EATING BAR

9' CLG.

PANTRY

OPTIONAL BASEMENT STAIRS

ARCH   ARCH

ARCH

DN

BEDROOM 2
10' X 9'8"

9' CLG.

LIVING ROOM
14'4" X 14'6"

VAULTED CEILING

ARCH

W
D

BEDROOM 3
10' X 9'8"

9' CLG.

PORCH

GARAGE
21'4" X 19'6"

42'

54'

© W. L. Martin Designs

As this one-story design proves, even small windows can have an impact when placed in the right spots.

the vanceboro

#50C ~8518 price code 19

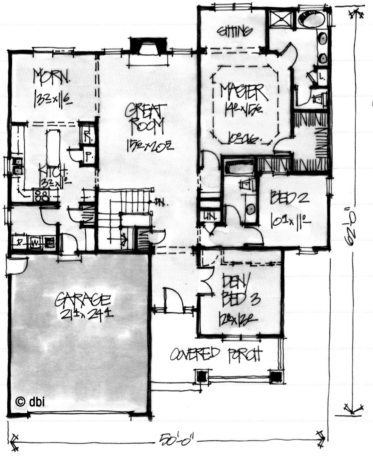

MORN.
13³x11⁶

GREAT ROOM
15⁶x20²

KITCH.
13³x11⁶

SITTING

MASTER
14⁸x15⁶

10⁸x16⁰

BED 2
10²x11⁰

DEN/ BED 3
12⁸x13⁸

GARAGE
21⁴x24⁴

© dbi

COVERED PORCH

50'-0"

62'-6"

Windows in an interesting shed dormer draw the eye upward.

1902 total sq. ft.

NOTE: 9 ft. main level walls

Windows enhance a home's sense of space, while providing dramatic focal points that draw the outdoors inside.

Photo Courtesy Of: Integrity® Windows and Doors

These photos are shown for example purposes only and are not from the inverness.

Photo By: John Stockwell

a study of home ~ the outside in & the inside out

When you order this plan you will receive a specification sheet for Integrity® Windows and Doors.

the inverness

#50C ~24043 price code 16

MASTER BEDROOM
14'6" X 12'4"
8' CLG.

DN

BEDROOM 2
12'6" X 10'4"
8' CLG.

OPEN TO BELOW

LIN

BEDROOM 3
12'6" X 10'4"
8' CLG.

8' CLG.

AC

42'

D W
AC

PANTRY

DINING ROOM
10'6" X 11'6

KITCHEN
10' X 11'6"

DN

EATING BAR
OPTIONAL BASEMENT STAIRS

GARAGE
20'6" X 20'4"

LIVING ROOM
16'10" X 17'6"

37'

UP

PORCH

© W. L. Martin Designs

731 main floor
901 second floor
1632 total sq. ft.
NOTE: 9 ft. main level walls

*three dormers give this home
a homey, nostalgic sense.*

When you order this plan you will receive a specification
sheet for Integrity® Windows and Doors.

the tahoe

#50C ~2537 price code 15

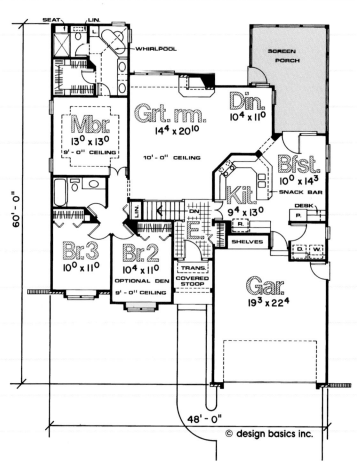

Here, a boxed window under
a pleasing gable becomes the front
elevation's primary focal point.

1580 total sq. ft.

a study of home ~ the outside in & the inside out

windows in special shapes & sizes

Because glass was a costly commodity at the time, early American homes featured considerably fewer and smaller windows than today's homes. As glass making techniques improved during the Industrial Revolution, costs decreased and the size and variety of window panes increased.

Today's window selection encompasses a number of shapes to suit our own unique tastes...from the ever-popular arch-topped windows and arched transoms, to octagons, pentagons, triangles and trapezoids.

Likewise, many of us choose large picture windows to paint an ever-changing mural. In rooms with soaring ceilings, it's common to stack windows on top of one another, flooding the space with light and beauty.

This photo is shown for example purposes only and is not from the silverdale.

© design basics inc.

When you order this plan you will receive a specification sheet for Integrity® Windows and Doors.

#50C ~6711
price code 14

the silverdale

A duet of stepped windows draw attention to the upper level of this home.

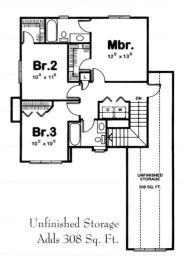

749 main floor
742 second floor
1491 total sq. ft.
NOTE: 9 ft. main level walls

Unfinished Storage
Adds 308 Sq. Ft.

design basics inc.
HOME PLAN DESIGN SERVICE
800-947-7526

the bedford

#50C ~2057 price code 22

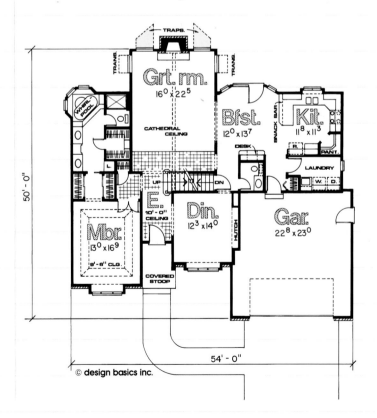

© design basics inc.

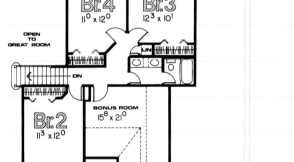

Unfinished Future Room
Adds 298 Sq. Ft.

1593 main floor
633 second floor

2226 total sq. ft.

Trapezoid transoms provide dramatic impact on either side of the great room's fireplace.

a study of home ~ the outside in & the inside out

When you order this plan you will receive a specification sheet for Integrity® Windows and Doors.

the marcell

#50C ~4133   price code 17

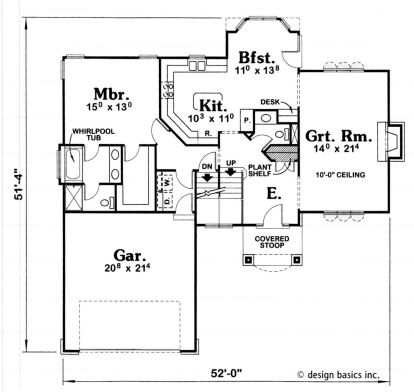

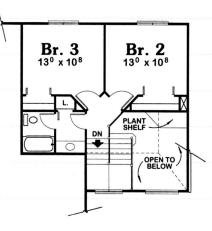

1314   main floor
458   second floor
1772   total sq. ft.

Triple-arch windows in the front and rear of the great room create impressive views.

800-947-7526

P. GERNANDT

the parnell

#50C ~3089
price code 17

A trio of gables and lovely arched windows gives this home a special flare.

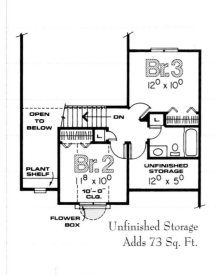

Br. 3
12⁰ x 10⁰

OPEN TO BELOW

DN

Br. 2
11⁸ x 10⁰
10'-0" CLG.

PLANT SHELF

UNFINISHED STORAGE
12⁰ x 5⁰

FLOWER BOX

Unfinished Storage Adds 73 Sq. Ft.

1316 main floor
396 second floor
1712 total sq. ft.

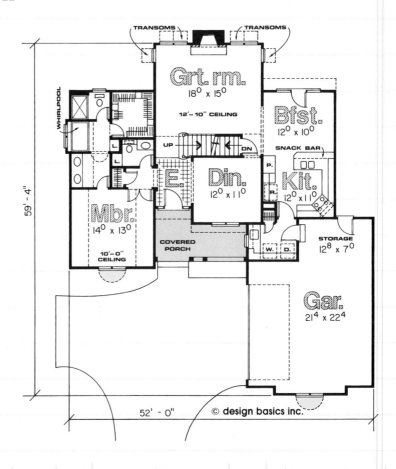

TRANSOMS   TRANSOMS

Grt. rm.
18⁰ x 15⁰

12'-10" CEILING

Bfst.
12⁰ x 10⁰

WHIRLPOOL

SNACK BAR

UP   DN

Din.
12⁰ x 11⁰

Kit.
12⁰ x 11⁰

P.

R.

Mbr.
14⁰ x 13⁰

10'-0" CEILING

59' - 4"

COVERED PORCH

W. D.

STORAGE
12⁸ x 7⁰

Gar.
21⁴ x 22⁴

52' - 0"

© design basics inc.

a study of home ~ the outside in & the inside out

These photos are shown for example purposes only and are not from the parnell.

Below:
A combination of different sized windows adds architectural interest to a pleasing view.

Above:
A triple window topped with a graceful arched transom lends a touch of drama to this dining room.

Right:
Sets of small, multi-paned windows give this kitchen a homey, nostalgic sense.

800-947-7526

HOME PLAN DESIGN SERVICE

Photos Courtesy Of: Integrity® Windows and Doors

When you order this plan you will receive a specification sheet for Integrity® Windows and Doors.

the philipsburg

#50C ~5520   price code 26

1955	main floor
660	second floor
2615	total sq. ft.

NOTE: 9 ft. main level walls

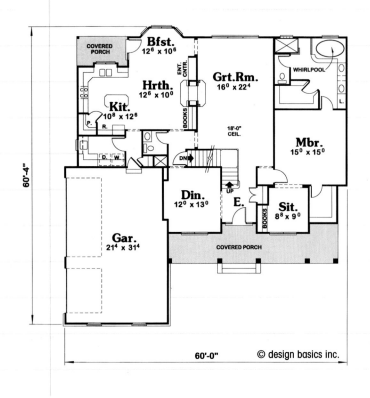

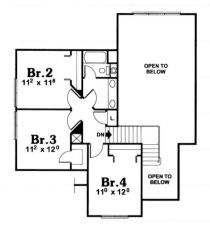

© design basics inc.

the different sizes of windows used on this home add variety and interest.

a study of home ~ the outside in & the inside out

These bayed windows are shown for example purposes only and are not from the aspen.

bayed, bowed
& boxed windows

Much like a ring provides a setting for jewels, these three design elements provide striking settings for windows. And just as a piece of jewelry accents a person's appearance, bayed, bowed or boxed windows become focal points on their homes' exteriors.

On the inside of the home, the deep ledge in front of a boxed window offers a picturesque setting for a lush collection of houseplants... or provides a perfect niche for a window seat—a cozy spot to sit and watch the rain or count the stars. Bayed windows are frequently used in sunny breakfast nooks, often adding extra room for tables and chairs. And adding a pair of overstuffed chairs in front of a great room's bowed window turns the space into a stunning conversation area.

1339 total sq. ft.

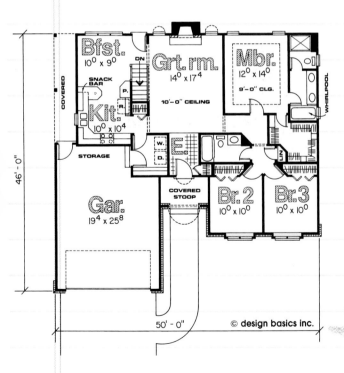

© design basics inc.

#50C ~3102
price code 13

the aspen

When you order this plan you will receive a specification sheet for Integrity® Windows and Doors.

A pair of gabled, boxed windows becomes the focus of attention on this pleasing elevation.

When you order this plan you will receive a specification sheet for Integrity® Windows and Doors.

the saratoga

#50C ~3316   price code 36

Unfinished Attic
Adds 892 Sq. Ft.

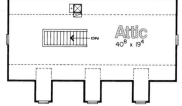

Attic
40⁸ x 19⁴

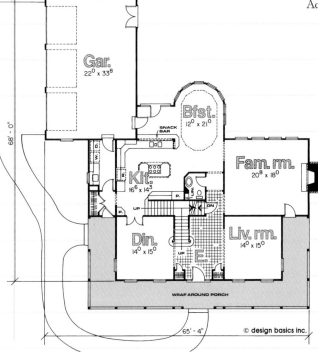

Gar.
22⁰ x 33⁸

Bfst.
12⁰ x 21⁰

SNACK BAR

Kit.
16⁶ x 14³

Fam. rm.
20⁸ x 18⁰

68' - 0"

Din.
14⁰ x 15⁰

Liv. rm.
14⁰ x 15⁰

WRAP AROUND PORCH

65' - 4"

© design basics inc.

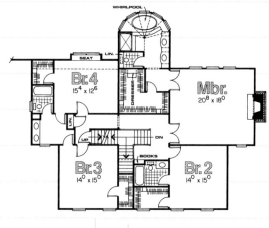

WHIRLPOOL

SEAT   LIN.

Br. 4
15⁴ x 12⁶

DRESSER

Mbr.
20⁸ x 18⁰

LIN.

UP

BOOKS

DN

Br. 3
14⁰ x 15⁰

Br. 2
14⁰ x 15⁰

1883	main floor
1801	second floor
3684	total sq. ft.

NOTE: 9 ft. main level walls

Multi-sided bayed windows add elegance in this gracious breakfast area and sumptuous master bath.

a study of home ~ the outside in & the inside out

the glendon

#50C ~8515   price code 23

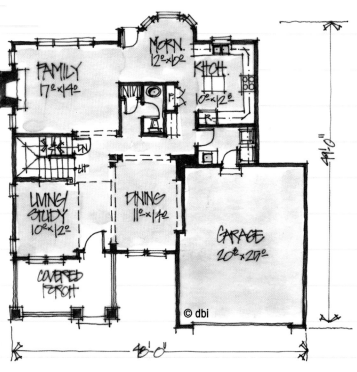

1207   main floor
1147   second floor
2354   total sq. ft.

NOTE: 9 ft. main level walls

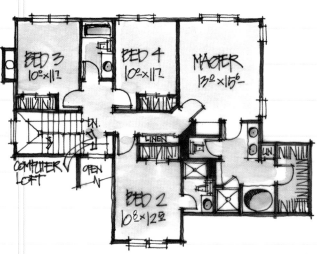

A bayed morning area offers a bright and sunny spot for everyday dining.

design basics inc. HOME PLAN DESIGN SERVICE   800-947-7526

27

When you order this plan you will receive a specification sheet for Integrity® Windows and Doors.

the kaitlyn

#50C ~5518 price code 22

Br.2 11⁰ x 12⁰

Br.3 10³ x 12⁰

Mbr. 13⁰ x 17⁰

9'-0" CEIL.

DN

L.

L.

WHIRLPOOL

Br.4 11⁰ x 10⁷

OPEN TO BELOW

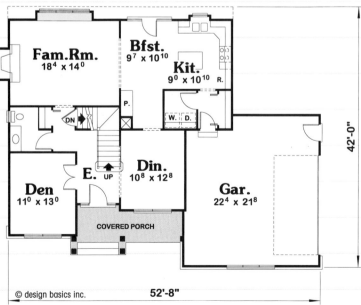

Fam.Rm. 18⁴ x 14⁰

Bfst. 9⁷ x 10¹⁰

Kit. 9⁰ x 10¹⁰

R.

P.

DN

W. D.

Den 11⁰ x 13⁰

E.

UP

Din. 10⁸ x 12⁸

Gar. 22⁴ x 21⁸

COVERED PORCH

42'-0"

© design basics inc.   52'-8"

1114	main floor
1165	second floor
2279	total sq. ft.

NOTE: 9 ft. main level walls

In the family room a triple wide boxed window creates a long window seat.

the tyndale

#50C ~2245 price code 16

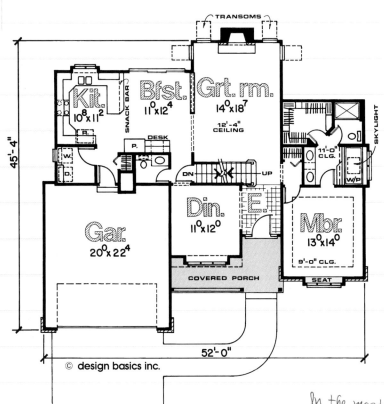

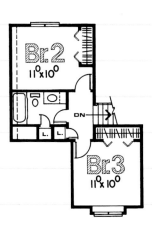

1297	main floor
388	second floor
1685	total sq. ft.

© design basics inc.

In the master bedroom, a boxed window seat offer a charming nook to sit in and gaze at the sky.

When you order this plan you will receive a specification sheet for Integrity® Windows and Doors.

the kensington

#50C   ~1864   price code 22

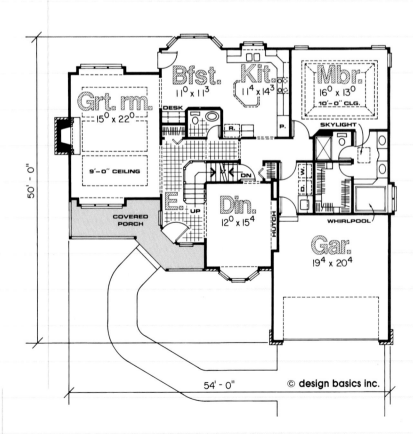

1553   main floor
725   second floor
2278   total sq. ft.

this nostalgic looking home enjoys a bayed dining room and a unique bayed entry.

a study of home ~ the outside in & the inside out

When you order this plan you will receive a specification
sheet for Integrity® Windows and Doors.

the hazelton

#50C ~1019 price code 22

1132	main floor
1087	second floor
2219	total sq. ft.

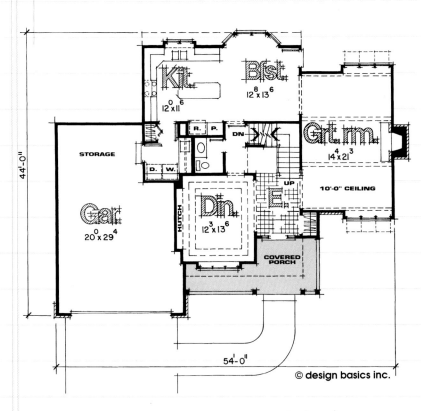

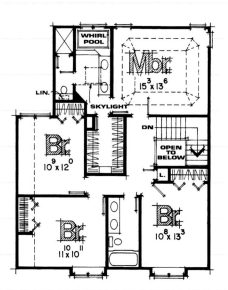

*Boxed windows adorn the front
and back of this home.*

© design basics inc.

When you order this plan you will receive a specification
sheet for Integrity® Windows and Doors.

the sarona

#50C   ~8526   price code 20

1025   main floor
1036   second floor
2061   total sq. ft.
NOTE: 9 ft. main level walls

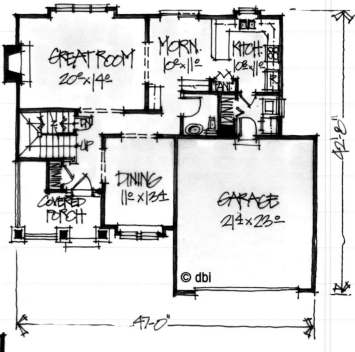

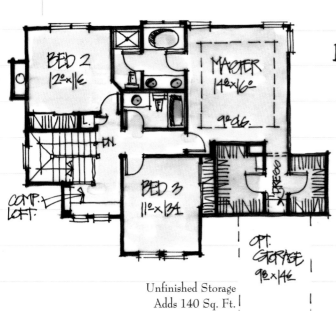

Unfinished Storage
Adds 140 Sq. Ft.

Plant lovers will appreciate the sunny niches created by boxed windows in the dining room, kitchen and great room.

a study of home ~ the outside in & the inside out

doors of glass

An increased use of glass in and around doors has also helped make today's homes more open, airy and light-filled. Transoms and sidelights framing a front door bathe any entry with warmth and hospitality. In the back of the home, a breakfast area may feature a sliding patio door that provides unrestricted views to a relaxing deck – without tying up any of the room's floor space.

On the inside of the home, elegant multi-light French doors between rooms allow living areas to be used separately or as one. They are also used to preserve acoustical privacy in home offices and dens while allowing a transfer of natural light and a sense of connection to the rest of the home.

This photo is shown for example purposes only and is not from the brooks.

Photo Courtesy Of: Integrity® Windows and Doors

A double window beside a set of French doors fills this living room with natural light.

#50C ~24020
price code 18

the brooks

When you order this plan you will receive a specification sheet for Integrity® Windows and Doors.

1819 total sq. ft.

NOTE: 9 ft. main level walls

design basics inc
HOME PLAN DESIGN SERVICE

800-947-7526

© W. L. Martin Designs

BEDROOM 2
12'8" X 10'6"
9' CLG.

NOOK
11'4" X 11'8"
9' CLG.

PORCH

HERS
LIN

DESK

EATING BAR

LIVING ROOM
15'10" X 18'6"
11' CLG.

HIS

KITCHEN
11'4" X 12'10"

MASTER BEDROOM
12'6" X 16'
11' CLG.

OVENS

BEDROOM 3
12'8" X 10'6"
9' CLG.

PANTRY

DINING ROOM
13'4" X 10'6"
9' CLG.

W
D

AC

STORAGE

DN

OPTIONAL BASEMENT STAIRS

PORCH

GARAGE
20'4" X 23'6"

54'

59'

When you order this plan you will receive a specification sheet for Integrity® Windows and Doors.

the cottondale

#50C ~24142   price code 24

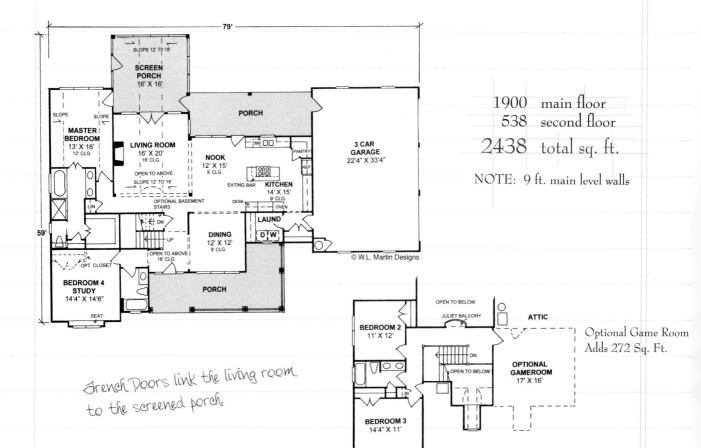

1900 main floor
538 second floor
2438 total sq. ft.

NOTE: 9 ft. main level walls

© W.L. Martin Designs

Optional Game Room
Adds 272 Sq. Ft.

French Doors link the living room to the screened porch.

a study of home ~ the outside in & the inside out

Photo Courtesy Of: Integrity® Windows and Doors

These photos are shown for example purposes only and are not from the cottondale.

Today's glass doors bring the surrounding natural beauty indoors. Combined with lovely transoms, views are further expanded.

design basics inc.
HOME PLAN DESIGN SERVICE

When you order this plan you will receive a specification sheet for Integrity® Windows and Doors.

the lagoda

#50C   ~24041   price code 39

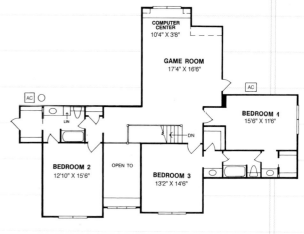

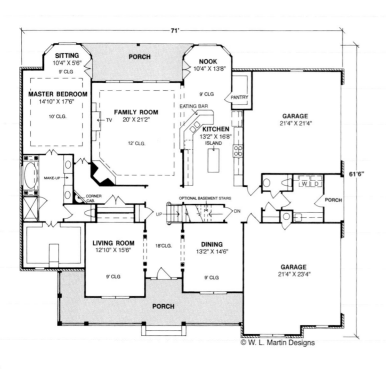

© W. L. Martin Designs

Both the master sitting area and the breakfast nook offer French doors leading to a private porch.

2472	main floor
1442	second floor
3914	**total sq. ft.**

NOTE: 9 ft. main level walls

a study of home ~ the outside in & the inside out

When you order this plan you will receive a specification sheet for Integrity® Windows and Doors.

the jennings

#50C ~3246   price code 26

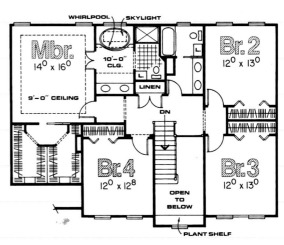

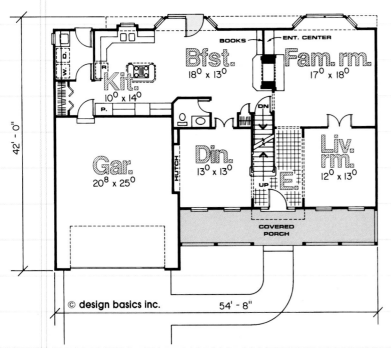

© design basics inc.   54' - 8"

42' - 0"

1366	main floor
1278	second floor
2644	total sq. ft.

In this bayed breakfast area, a garden door offers access to the backyard without obstructing the view.

Photo Courtesy Of: Integrity® Windows and Doors

This kitchen is shown for example purposes only and is not from the la crosse.

improved window technology

While homeowners' desires for light-laden homes have grown, improved technology has made the use of larger sizes and numbers of windows more feasible. Today's tempered glass resists breakage. Special low emissivity coatings reduce heat transference and UV coatings reduce furniture fading. Advanced weather stripping materials and techniques insulate better than ever. And improved window and door locking mechanisms protect the inside from threats from the outside.

1724 total sq. ft.

NOTE: 9 ft. main level walls

#50C ~8527
price code 17

the la crosse

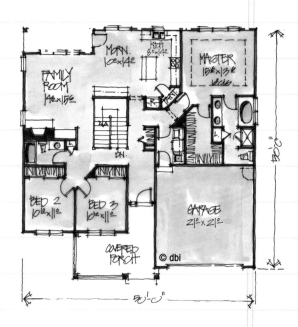

When you order this plan you will receive a specification sheet for Integrity® Windows and Doors.

Thanks to today's energy efficient windows, this master bedroom's triple wide windows are warm and draft-free.

the briarton

#50C ~5503 price code 25

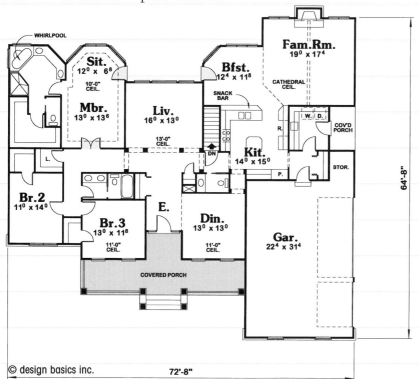

2586 total sq. ft.

NOTE: 9 ft. main level walls

© design basics inc.

Advancements in technology have made it more practical to have an abundance of windows as found on the back of this home.

the bridgeland

#50C ~8523 price code 20

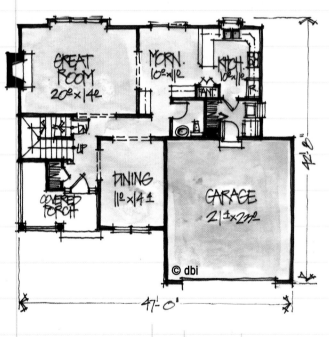

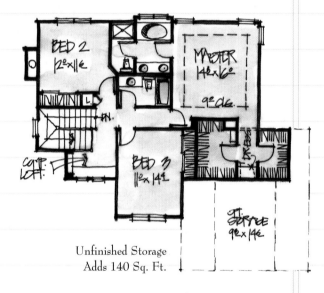

Unfinished Storage
Adds 140 Sq. Ft.

1036 main floor
1048 second floor

2084 total sq. ft.

NOTE: 9 ft. main level walls

this great room's group of boxed windows brings in lots of natural light - without sacrificing energy costs.

When you order this plan you will receive a specification sheet for Marvin® Windows and Doors.

#50C ~1752
price code 18

lancaster

this 2-story entry offers a generous coat closet topped with charming plant shelf and bent staircase.

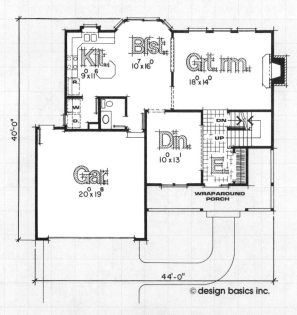

© design basics inc.

40'-0"
44'-0"

Kit 9⁰ x 11⁰
Bfst 10⁷ x 16⁰
Grt rm. 18⁰ x 14⁰
Dn 10⁰ x 13⁰
Gar 20⁰ x 19⁸
WRAPAROUND PORCH

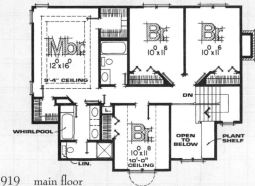

Mbr 12 x 16
Br 10⁰ x 11⁶
Br 10⁰ x 11⁶
Br 10⁰ x 11⁰ 10'-0" CEILING
9'-4" CEILING
WHIRLPOOL
LIN.
OPEN TO BELOW
PLANT SHELF
DN

919   main floor
927   second floor
1846   total sq. ft.

When you order this plan you will receive a specification sheet for Marvin® Windows and Doors.

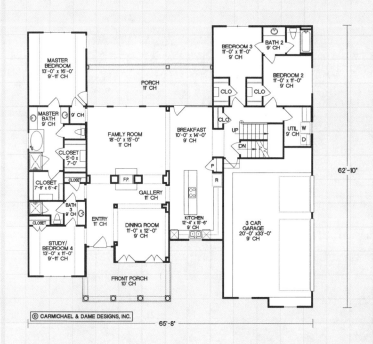

© CARMICHAEL & DAME DESIGNS, INC.

62'-10"
65'-8"

MASTER BEDROOM 13'-0" x 16'-0" 9'-11" CH
PORCH 11' CH
BEDROOM 3 11'-0" x 11'-0" 9' CH
BATH 2 9' CH
BEDROOM 2 11'-0" x 11'-0" 9' CH
MASTER BATH 9' CH
CLO
CLO
CLO
FAMILY ROOM 18'-0" x 15'-0" 11' CH
BREAKFAST 10'-0" x 14'-0" 9' CH
UTIL 9' CH
CLOSET 5'-0 x 7'-0
CLOSET 7'-8 x 6'-4
CLOSET
UP
DN
GALLERY 11' CH
KITCHEN 12'-4 x 15'-6 9' CH
3 CAR GARAGE 20'-0" x33'-0" 9' CH
BATH 3 9' CH
ENTRY 11' CH
DINING ROOM 11'-0" x 12'-0" 9' CH
STUDY / BEDROOM 4 13'-0" x 11'-0" 9'-11" CH
FRONT PORCH 10' CH

2393   total sq. ft.
NOTE: 9 ft. main level walls

UNFINISHED BONUS ROOM 12'-4 x 18'-0 9' CH
DN
8' CH

Unfinished Future Space
Adds 222 Sq. Ft.

this long eating bar will seat the whole family for breakfast, or offer extra seating when entertaining.

#50C ~5149

price code 21

camrose

When you order this plan you will receive a specification sheet for Marvin® Windows and Doors.

When you order this plan you will receive a specification sheet for Marvin® Windows and Doors.

#50C ~1330

price code 18

trenton

Tall transom-topped windows and a volume ceiling make this great room very open and airy.

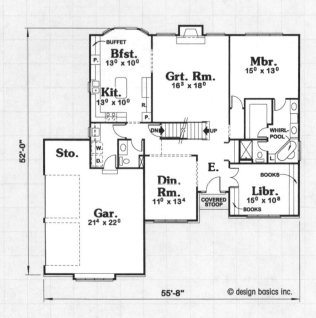

BUFFET

P.

Bfst.
13⁰ x 10⁰

Kit.
13⁰ x 10⁰

Grt. Rm.
16³ x 18⁰

Mbr.
15⁰ x 13⁰

R.

P.

DN↓ ↑UP

WHIRL-POOL

52'-0"

Sto.

W.
D.

Gar.
21⁴ x 22⁰

Din. Rm.
11⁰ x 13⁴

E.

COVERED STOOP

BOOKS

Libr.
15⁰ x 10⁸

BOOKS

L

55'-8"

© design basics inc.

A triple window makes this library bright and cheery while built-in bookshelves add convenience.

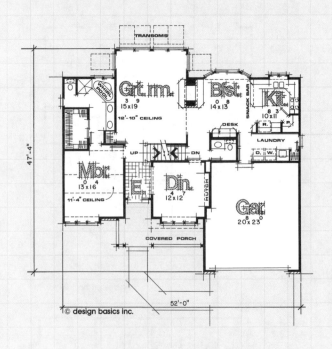

TRANSOMS

WHIRL POOL

Grt. rm.
3 9
15x19
12'-10" CEILING

Bfst.
14x13

SNACK BAR

Kit.
8 3
10x11
R.

DESK

47'-4"

UP→ ←DN

LAUNDRY

D. W.

Mbr.
0 4
13x16
11'-4" CEILING

E.

Din.
4 7
12x12

HUTCH

Gar.
20 x 23⁰

COVERED PORCH

52'-0"

© design basics inc.

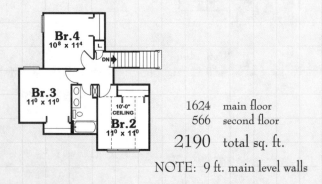

Br.4
10⁸ x 11⁴

L

DN↓

Br.3
11⁰ x 11⁰

10'-0" CEILING

Br.2
11⁰ x 11⁰

1624   main floor
566   second floor

2190   total sq. ft.

NOTE: 9 ft. main level walls

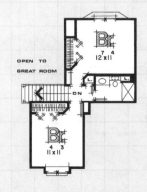

Br.
7 4
12 x 11

OPEN TO GREAT ROOM

←DN

Br.
4 3
11 x 11

1421   main floor
448   second floor

1869   total sq. ft.

a study of home ~ the outside in & the inside out

When you order this plan you will receive a specification sheet for Marvin® Windows and Doors.

#50C ~1539
price code 19

mansfield

Transom-topped windows in the great room and breakfast area flood the casual living areas with light.

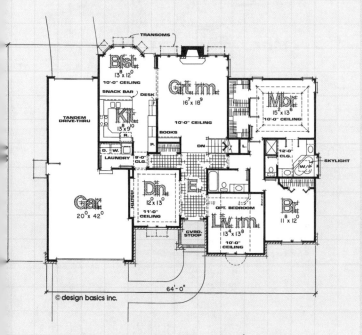

© design basics inc.

1996 total sq. ft.

ALL PLANS HAVE BEEN REGISTERED
ORIGINAL C DRAFT
WITH THE U.S. COPYRIGHT OFFICE

#50C ~2312
price code 21

meredith

When you order this plan you will receive a specification sheet for Marvin® Windows and Doors.

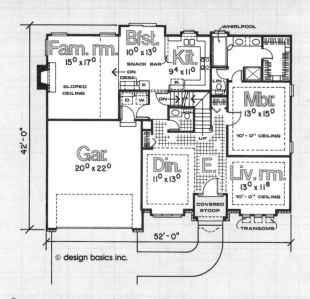

© design basics inc.

Overlooking the family room, this second floor loft could be used as a home office or an additional bedroom.

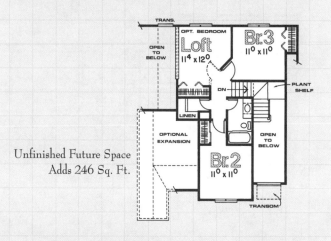

Unfinished Future Space
Adds 246 Sq. Ft.

1519	main floor
594	second floor
2113	total sq. ft.

#50C ~24044
price code 18
farrelton

Shared space between the kitchen and breakfast nook allows guests to mingle without feeling cramped.

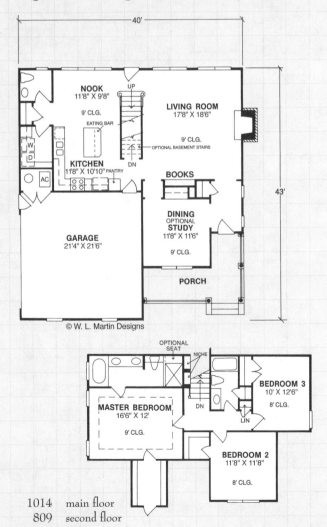

40'

NOOK
11'8" X 9'8"
9' CLG.

UP

LIVING ROOM
17'8" X 18'6"
9' CLG.

EATING BAR

W
D

KITCHEN
11'8" X 10'10" PANTRY

AC

DN

OPTIONAL BASEMENT STAIRS

BOOKS

DINING
OPTIONAL
STUDY
11'8" X 11'6"
9' CLG.

GARAGE
21'4" X 21'6"

43'

PORCH

© W. L. Martin Designs

OPTIONAL SEAT

NICHE

MASTER BEDROOM
16'6" X 12'
9' CLG.

DN

BEDROOM 3
10' X 12'6"
8' CLG.

LIN

BEDROOM 2
11'8" X 11'8"
8' CLG.

1014 main floor
809   second floor
1823 total sq. ft.

NOTE: 9 ft. main level walls

#50C ~6740
price code 11
balentine

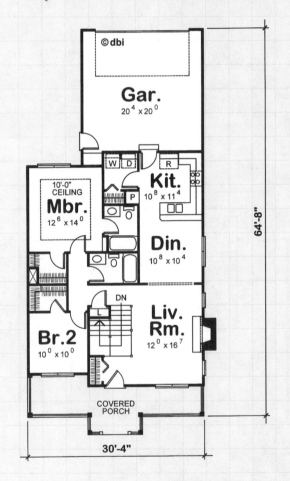

© dbi

Gar.
20⁴ x 20⁰

W D

R

Kit.
10⁸ x 11⁴

10'-0"
CEILING
Mbr.
12⁶ x 14⁰

P

Din.
10⁸ x 10⁴

DN

Br.2
10⁰ x 10⁰

Liv.
Rm.
12⁰ x 16⁷

64'-8"

COVERED
PORCH

30'-4"

1142 total sq. ft.
NOTE: 9 ft. main level walls

Both the master and secondary bedrooms enjoy walk-in closets.

a study of home ~ the outside in & the inside out

#50C ~1551
price code 12

logan

#50C ~6750
price code 13

aiken

An open floor plan offers a view of the lovely fireplace from the kitchen and dining area.

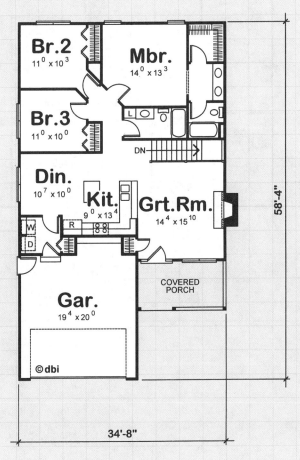

Br.2 11⁰ x 10³
Mbr. 14⁰ x 13³
Br.3 11⁰ x 10⁰
DN
Din. 10⁷ x 10⁰
Kit. 9⁰ x 13⁴
Grt.Rm. 14⁴ x 15¹⁰
W D R
Gar. 19⁴ x 20⁰
COVERED PORCH
©dbi
58'-4"
34'-8"

1311 total sq. ft.
NOTE: 9 ft. main level walls

TRAPS.
Mbr. 12 x 13 9'-0" CEILING
Grt.rm. 14⁰ x 20³ CATHEDRAL CEILING
Din. 11 x 11⁶
DESK
SNACK BAR
W. D.
Br. 10 x 11
Br. 10³ x 10⁰
Kit. 10 x 10⁰
DN
COVERED STOOP.
Gar. 19⁴ x 21⁴
46'-0"
50'-0"
© design basics inc.

1271 total sq. ft.

A soaring cathedral ceiling and a fireplace flanked by windows make this a beautiful great room.

design basics inc.
HOME PLAN DESIGN SERVICE
800-947-7526

45

#50C ~24009

wainright
price code 24

#50C ~1767

rosebury
price code 16

The upper level includes a loft, ideal for a desk and computer, plus a space for an optional game room.

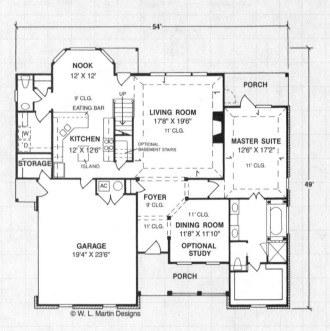

© W. L. Martin Designs

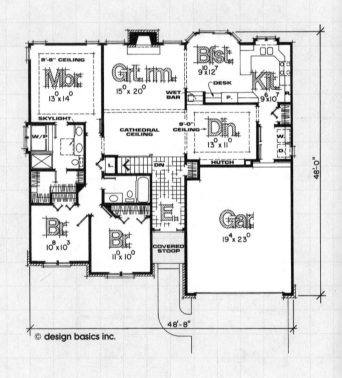

© design basics inc.

1604 total sq. ft.

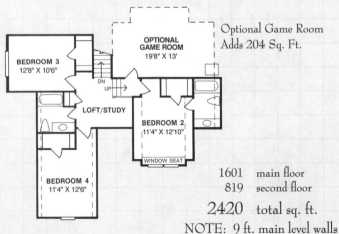

Optional Game Room Adds 204 Sq. Ft.

1601 main floor
819 second floor
2420 total sq. ft.
NOTE: 9 ft. main level walls

A built-in desk, a pantry and a wet bar add convenience in the breakfast area.

a study of home ~ the outside in & the inside out

When you order this plan you will receive a specification sheet for Marvin® Windows and Doors.

#50C ~2526

price code 16

arbor

A ceiling that slopes to nearly 17 feet creates a dramatic great room.

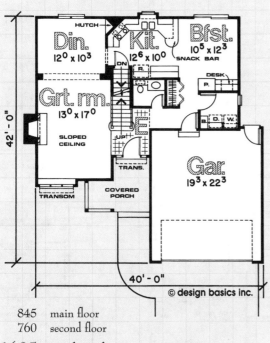

845 main floor
760 second floor
1605 total sq. ft.

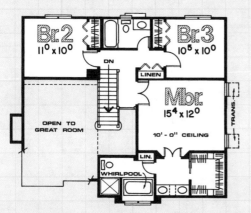

When you order this plan you will receive a specification sheet for Marvin® Windows and Doors.

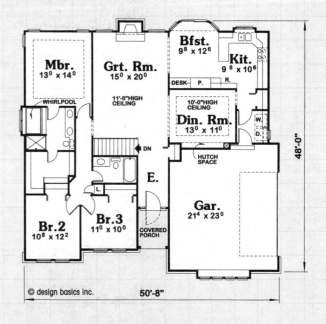

1650 total sq. ft.
NOTE: 9 ft. main level walls

A 10-foot-high ceiling and a recessed hutch space bring style to this formal dining room.

design basics inc.
HOME PLAN DESIGN SERVICE
800-947-7526

#50C ~1553
price code 23

kendall

When you order this plan you will receive a specification sheet for Marvin® Windows and Doors.

When you order this plan you will receive a specification sheet for Marvin® Windows and Doors.

#50C ~24038
price code 21

clarkson

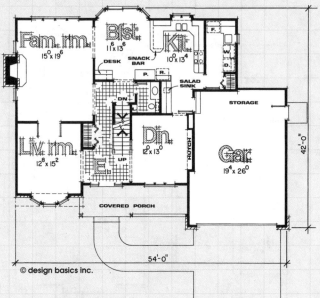

Fam. rm.
15'0 x 19'6

Bfst.
11'6 x 13'6

Kit.
10'0 x 13'4

DESK

SNACK
BAR

P. R.

SALAD
SINK

STORAGE

DN

Liv. rm.
12'8 x 15'2

UP

Dn.
12 x 13'0

HUTCH

Gar.
19'4 x 26'0

42'-0"

COVERED PORCH

© design basics inc.

54'-0"

French doors connect the living and family rooms for added flexibility.

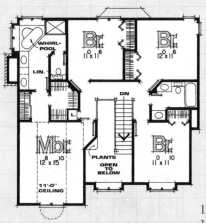

WHIRL-POOL

LIN.

Br.
11 x 11

Br.
12'0 x 11'6

DN

Mbr.
12'8 x 15'10

PLANTS
OPEN TO
BELOW

Br.
11'0 x 10

11'-0"
CEILING

1303   main floor
1084   second floor
2387   total sq. ft.

A built-in entertainment center in the family room offers a place for home electronics.

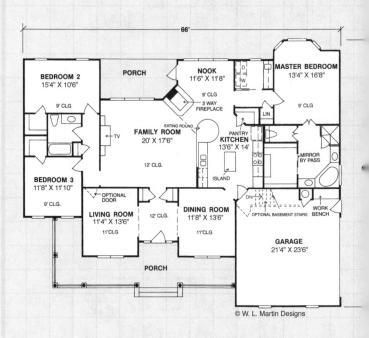

66'

BEDROOM 2
15'4" X 10'6"
9' CLG

PORCH

NOOK
11'6" X 11'8"
9' CLG

MASTER BEDROOM
13'4" X 16'8"
9' CLG

3 WAY
FIREPLACE

EATING ROUND

FAMILY ROOM
20' X 17'6"
12' CLG.

TV

BEDROOM 3
11'8" X 11'10"
9' CLG.

PANTRY

KITCHEN
13'6" X 14'

ISLAND

LIN

MIRROR
BY PASS

OPTIONAL
DOOR

DN

OPTIONAL BASEMENT STAIRS

WORK
BENCH

LIVING ROOM
11'4" X 13'6"
11'CLG

12' CLG.

DINING ROOM
11'8" X 13'6"
11'CLG

GARAGE
21'4" X 23'6"

PORCH

© W. L. Martin Designs

2126   total sq. ft.

NOTE: 9 ft. main level walls

a study of home ~ the outside in & the inside out

When you order this plan you will receive a specification sheet for Integrity® Windows and Doors.

#50C ~8045
price code 21

coopers farm

#50C ~2235
price code 19

albany

When you order this plan you will receive a specification sheet for Marvin® Windows and Doors.

A built-in desk in the breakfast area provides a place for menu-planning, homework or computer games.

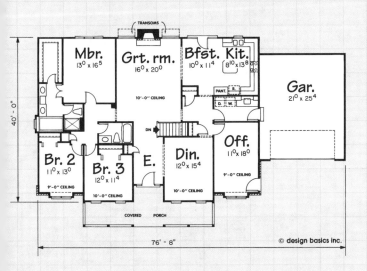

2151 total sq. ft.

With its own outside entrance, this home office is ideal for meeting with clients.

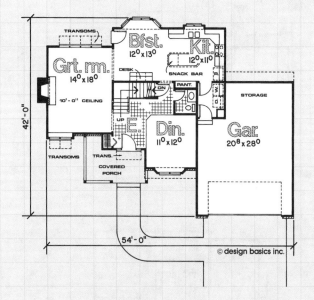

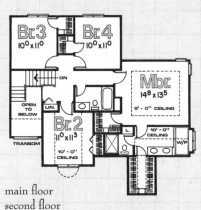

944 main floor
987 second floor

1931 total sq. ft.

design basics inc. HOME PLAN DESIGN SERVICE 800-947-7526

49

#50C ~8038
price code 24

stone creek

#50C ~2206
price code 24

hawkesbury

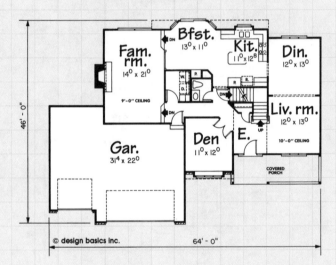

Special ceiling detail makes this breakfast area feel like a gazebo.

Fam. rm. 14⁰ x 21⁰ — 9'-0" CEILING

Bfst. 13⁰ x 11⁰

Kit. 11⁰ x 12⁸

Din. 12⁰ x 13⁰

Liv. rm. 12⁰ x 13⁰ — 10'-0" CEILING

Den 11⁰ x 12⁰

Gar. 31⁴ x 22⁰

46' - 0"

64' - 0"

COVERED PORCH

E.

© design basics inc.

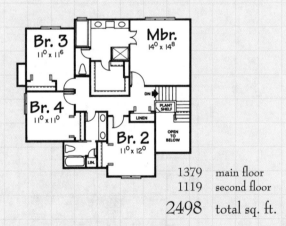

Br. 3 11⁰ x 11⁶

Mbr. 14⁰ x 14⁸

Br. 4 11⁰ x 11⁰

Br. 2 11⁰ x 12⁰

PLANT SHELF

LINEN

OPEN TO BELOW

1379   main floor
1119   second floor
2498   total sq. ft.

Having the family room a few steps lower than the rest of the main floor gives it a sense of intimacy.

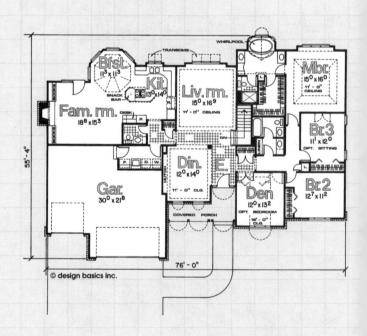

Bfst. 11⁹ x 11³

Kit. 13⁰ x 14⁰

Fam. rm. 18⁸ x 15³

Liv. rm. 15⁰ x 16⁹ — 11'-0" CEILING

Mbr. 15⁰ x 16⁰ — 11'-0" CEILING

Br 3 11⁴ x 12⁰ OPT. SITTING

Br. 2 12⁷ x 11²

Din. 12⁰ x 14⁰

Gar. 30⁰ x 21⁸

Den 12⁰ x 13² OPT. BEDROOM

COVERED PORCH

WHIRLPOOL

TRANSOMS

SNACK BAR

DESK

E.

55' - 4"

76' - 0"

© design basics inc.

2498   total sq. ft.

a study of home ~ the outside in & the inside out

When you order this plan you will receive a specification sheet for Marvin® Windows and Doors.

#50C ~24021

price code 19

barber

A bayed sitting area turns the master suite into a great getaway.

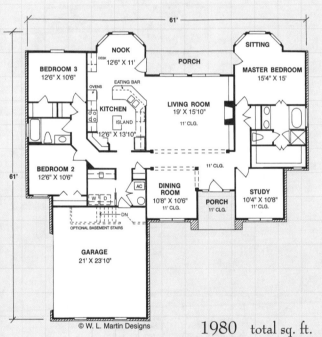

61'

NOOK
12'6" X 11'

PORCH

SITTING

MASTER BEDROOM
15'4" X 15'

BEDROOM 3
12'6" X 10'6"

OVENS

EATING BAR

KITCHEN
12'6" X 13'10"

ISLAND

DESK

LIVING ROOM
19' X 15'10"
11' CLG.

BEDROOM 2
12'6" X 10'6"

61'

W D

AC

DN

OPTIONAL BASEMENT STAIRS

DINING ROOM
10'8" X 10'6"
11' CLG.

PORCH
11' CLG.

STUDY
10'4" X 10'8"
11' CLG.

11' CLG.

GARAGE
21' X 23'10"

© W. L. Martin Designs

1980 total sq. ft.

NOTE: 9 ft. main level walls

#50C ~8520

price code 22

mindoro

When you order this plan you will receive a specification sheet for Marvin® Windows and Doors.

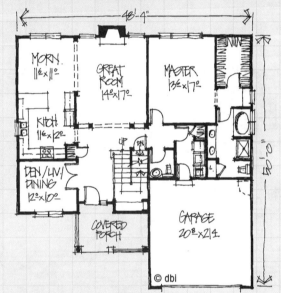

48'-4"

50'-0"

MORN.
11'6 x 11'0

GREAT ROOM
14'6 x 17'0

MASTER
13'6 x 17'0

KITCH.
11'6 x 12'0

DEN/LIV./DINING
12'6 x 10'0

COVERED PORCH

GARAGE
20'8 x 21'4

© dbi

On the second level, a computer loft with built-in bookcase is sure to be well-used.

OPEN

OPEN

BOOKS

BED 4
10'8 x 10'8

COMP. LOFT

BED 3
10'8 x 10'8

SEAT

BED 2
10'8 x 11'8

1538 main floor
680 second floor

2218 total sq. ft.

NOTE: 9 ft. main level walls

design basics inc.
HOME PLAN DESIGN SERVICE

800-947-7526

51

churchill

When you order this plan you will receive a specification sheet for Marvin® Windows and Doors.

When you order this plan you will receive a specification sheet for Marvin® Windows and Doors.

leawood

#50C ~2779
price code 26

transom-topped windows and an 11-foot-high spider-beamed ceiling produce a stylish den

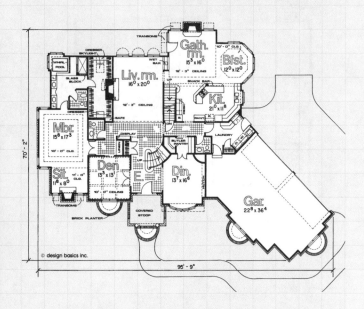

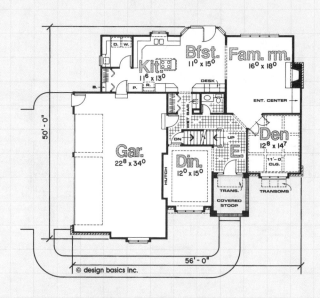

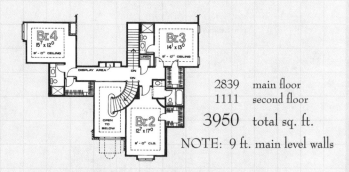

2839 main floor
1111 second floor

3950 total sq. ft.

NOTE: 9 ft. main level walls

This spectacular 2-story entry showcases a floating, curved staircase.

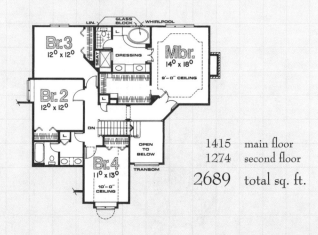

1415 main floor
1274 second floor

2689 total sq. ft.

When you order this plan you will receive a specification sheet for Marvin® Windows and Doors.

#50C ~8510

price code 26

wilkesboro

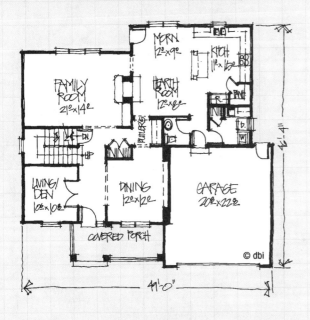

The butler's pantry next to the dining room saves steps when entertaining.

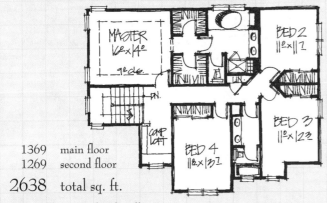

1369   main floor
1269   second floor
2638   total sq. ft.

NOTE: 9 ft. main level walls

#50C ~2476

price code 28

dundee

When you order this plan you will receive a specification sheet for Marvin® Windows and Doors.

A row of bowed, transom-topped windows and a volume ceiling create a stunning great room.

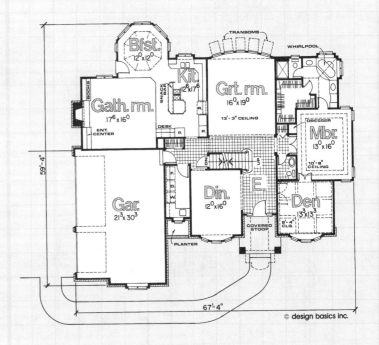

2183   main floor
701   second floor
2884   total sq. ft.

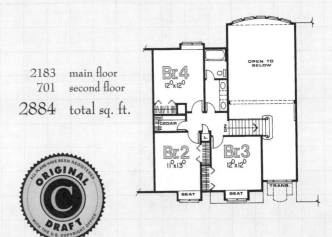

design basics inc. — HOME PLAN DESIGN SERVICE — 800-947-7526

jennys brook

When you order this plan you will receive a specification sheet for Integrity® Windows and Doors.

The master suite is separated from the secondary bedrooms for added privacy.

1691   total sq. ft.

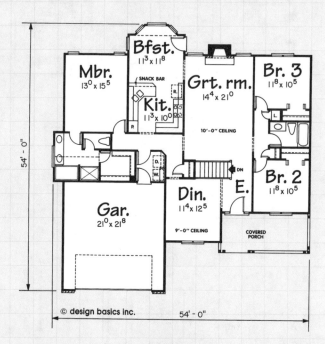

#50C ~1862

price code 23

manchester

When you order this plan you will receive a specification sheet for Marvin® Windows and Doors.

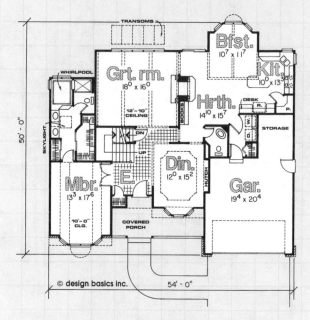

1653   main floor
700   second floor
2353   total sq. ft.

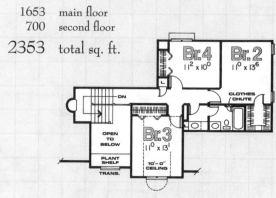

French doors lead to a beautiful master bedroom with lovely bayed windows and unique angled ceiling.

a study of home ~ the outside in & the inside out

When you order this plan you will receive a specification sheet for Marvin® Windows and Doors.

#50C ~1748
price code 19 sinclair

#50C ~2309
price code 25 edmonton

When you order this plan you will receive a specification sheet for Marvin® Windows and Doors.

A see-thru fireplace spreads warmth in the great room and hearth room.

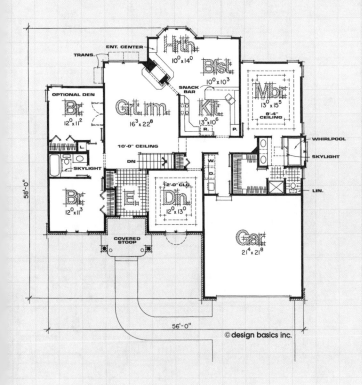

1911   total sq. ft.

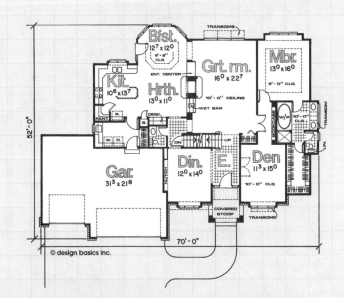

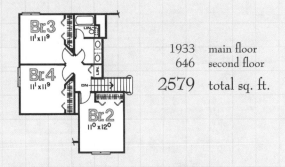

1933   main floor
646   second floor
2579   total sq. ft.

French doors lead to a private hall which links the master suite and den and features a generous bookcase.

design basics inc.
HOME PLAN DESIGN SERVICE
800-947-7526

When you order this plan you will receive a specification sheet for Marvin® Windows and Doors.

#50C ~3385

price code 17

brittany

the sunny, bowed breakfast area includes
a garden door to the back yard.

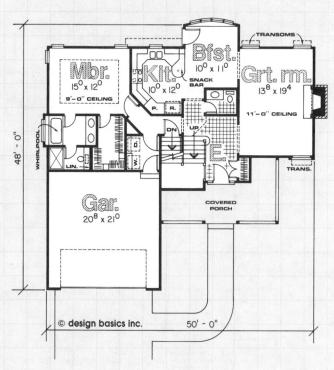

1191   main floor
597   second floor
1788   total sq. ft.

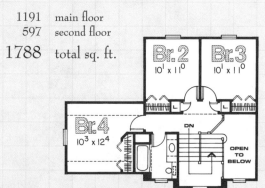

#50C ~8084

price code 18

brook valley

When you order this plan you will receive a specification sheet for Marvin® Windows or Doors.

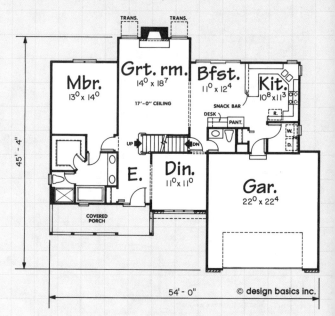

A soaring 17-foot-high ceiling and a fireplace
flanked by transom-topped windows set this
great room apart.

1301   main floor
564   second floor
1865   total sq. ft.

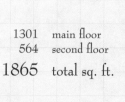
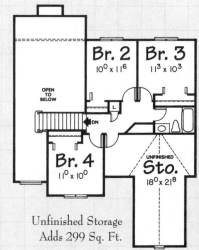

Unfinished Storage
Adds 299 Sq. Ft.

a study of home ~ the outside in & the inside out

When you order this plan you will receive a specification sheet for Integrity® Windows and Doors.

#50C ~6715
price code 14

sycamoor

A gracious front entry includes a window seat and views of an open staircase and the formal living room.

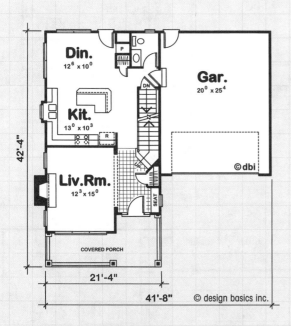

Din.
12⁶ x 10⁰

P

Gar.
20⁰ x 25⁴

Kit.
13⁰ x 10³

DN

R

42'-4"

Liv.Rm.
12³ x 15⁰

©dbi

SEAT

COVERED PORCH

21'-4"

41'-8"   © design basics inc.

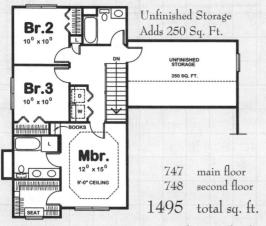

Br.2
10⁰ x 10⁰

Unfinished Storage
Adds 250 Sq. Ft.

DN

UNFINISHED
STORAGE
250 SQ. FT.

Br.3
10⁰ x 10⁰

D

W

BOOKS

Mbr.
12⁰ x 15⁰
9'-0" CEILING

SEAT

747   main floor
748   second floor
1495   total sq. ft.

NOTE: 9 ft. main level walls

#50C ~24126
price code 14

bellglade

When you order this plan you will receive a specification sheet for Integrity® Windows or Doors.

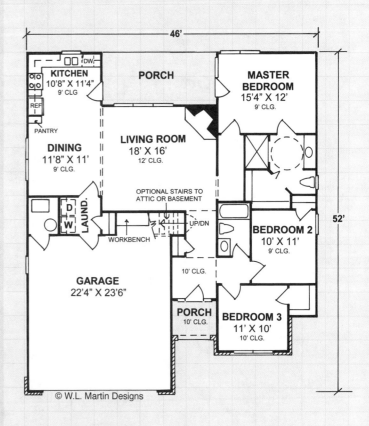

46'

DW

KITCHEN
10'8" X 11'4"
9' CLG.

PORCH

MASTER
BEDROOM
15'4" X 12'
9' CLG.

REF

PANTRY

DINING
11'8" X 11'
9' CLG.

LIVING ROOM
18' X 16'
12' CLG.

OPTIONAL STAIRS TO
ATTIC OR BASEMENT

52'

D
W

LAUND.

UP/DN

BEDROOM 2
10' X 11'
9' CLG.

WORKBENCH

GARAGE
22'4" X 23'6"

10' CLG.

PORCH
10' CLG.

BEDROOM 3
11' X 10'
10' CLG.

© W.L. Martin Designs

UNIVERSAL DESIGN

1407   total sq. ft.

NOTE: 9 ft. main level walls

Wide hallways and doors, a spacious master bath and an open floor plan make this Universal Design highly accessible.

#50C ~8091

price code 13

winter woods

When you order this plan you will receive a specification sheet for Integrity® Windows and Doors.

When you order this plan you will receive a specification sheet for Integrity® Windows and Doors.

#50C ~6705

price code 16

hopewell

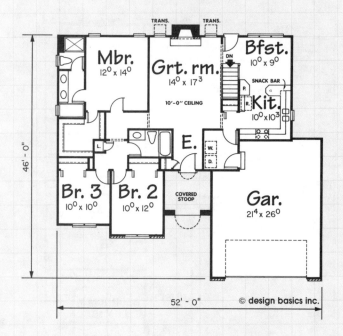

Mbr. 12⁰ x 14⁰

Grt. rm. 14⁰ x 17³

10'-0" CEILING

Bfst. 10⁰ x 9⁰

SNACK BAR

Kit. 10⁰ x 10³

TRANS.   TRANS.

DN

E.

W. D.

Br. 3 10⁰ x 10⁰

Br. 2 10⁰ x 12⁰

COVERED STOOP

Gar. 21⁴ x 26⁰

46' - 0"

52' - 0"

© design basics inc.

1360   total sq. ft.

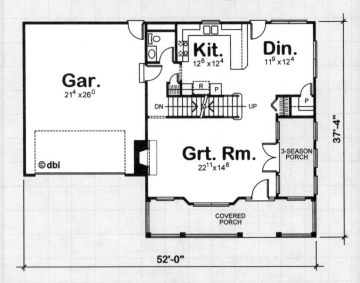

Gar. 21⁴ x 26⁰

Kit. 12⁶ x 12⁴

Din. 11⁹ x 12⁴

DN   R P   UP

P

Grt. Rm. 22¹¹ x 14⁸

3-SEASON PORCH

COVERED PORCH

© dbi

37'-4"

52'-0"

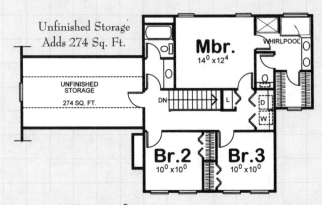

Unfinished Storage
Adds 274 Sq. Ft.

UNFINISHED STORAGE

274 SQ. FT.

Mbr. 14⁰ x 12⁴

WHIRLPOOL

DN   L

D W

Br. 2 10⁰ x 10⁰

Br. 3 10⁰ x 10⁰

846   main floor
804   second floor

1650   total sq. ft.

NOTE: 9 ft. main level walls

the entry presents a striking view to the great room's fireplace flanked by transom-topped windows.

a 3-season porch off the great room is a delightful spot to bask in sunlight.

a study of home ~ the outside in & the inside out

When you order this plan you will receive a specification sheet for Integrity® Windows and Doors.

#50C ~24003

price code 17

tuxford

An 11-foot-high, vaulted ceiling and a wall of windows create an expansive family room.

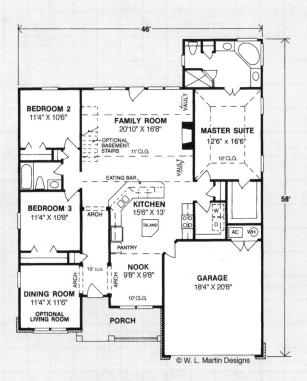

© W. L. Martin Designs

1762 total sq. ft.

NOTE: 9 ft. main level walls

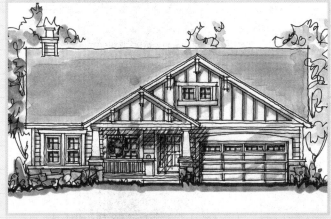

When you order this plan you will receive a specification sheet for Integrity® Windows and Doors.

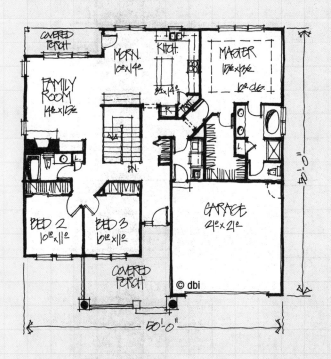

© dbi

1724 total sq. ft.

NOTE: 9 ft. main level walls

A secluded hallway leads to a private master suite.

#50C ~8500
price code 22

castalia

When you order this plan you will receive a specification sheet for Integrity® Windows and Doors.

#50C ~3121
price code 16

bellamy

When you order this plan you will receive a specification sheet for Integrity® Windows and Doors.

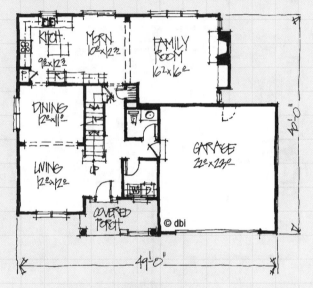

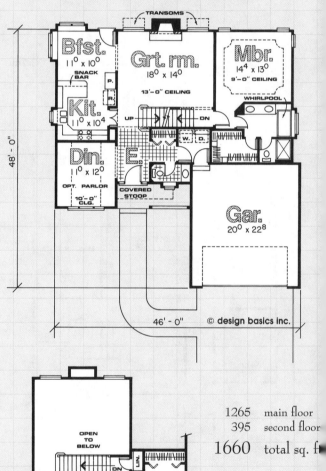

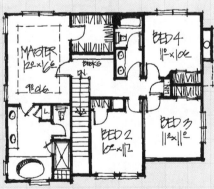

1130 main floor
1070 second floor

2200 total sq. ft.

NOTE: 9 ft. main level walls

1265 main floor
395   second floor

1660 total sq. f

A large bookcase on the upstairs landing provides plenty of space for bedtime reading materials.

A vaulted ceiling and a triple window create a handsome dining room.

a study of home ~ the outside in & the inside out

When you order this plan you will receive a specification sheet for Integrity® Windows and Doors.

#50C ~8037
price code 18

carriage hills

A soaring ceiling enhances the great room's sense of spaciousness.

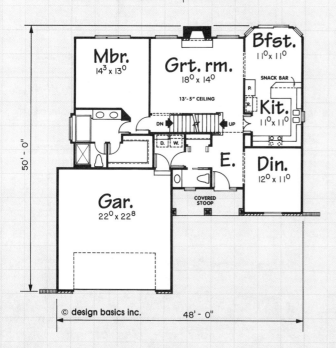

- Mbr. 14³ x 13⁰
- Grt. rm. 18⁰ x 14⁰
- 13'-5" CEILING
- Bfst. 11⁰ x 11⁰
- SNACK BAR
- Kit. 11⁰ x 11⁰
- E.
- Din. 12⁰ x 11⁰
- COVERED STOOP
- Gar. 22⁰ x 22⁸
- DN
- UP
- D. W.
- 50' - 0"
- 48' - 0"

© design basics inc.

1284	main floor
518	second floor
1802	**total sq. ft.**

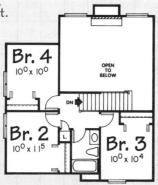

- Br. 4 10⁰ x 10⁰
- OPEN TO BELOW
- DN
- Br. 2 10⁰ x 11⁵
- Br. 3 10⁰ x 10⁴

When you order this plan you will receive a specification sheet for Integrity® Windows and Doors.

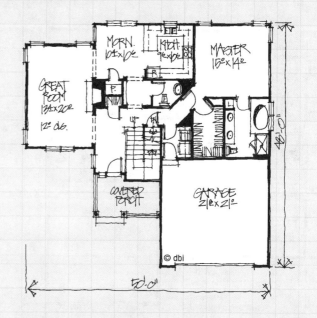

- MORN. 10⁴ x 10⁰
- KIT. 9⁶ x 10⁶
- MASTER 15⁰ x 14²
- GREAT ROOM 13⁴ x 20⁰
- 12⁰ clg.
- UP
- COVERED PORCH
- GARAGE 21⁸ x 21⁰
- 46'-0"
- 50'-0"

© dbi

- BED 3 10⁸ x 11⁸
- BED 2 10⁸ x 11⁸
- COMPUTER LOFT
- DN
- LIN.
- BED 4 10⁴ x 12⁴
- OPEN

1302	main floor
757	second floor
2059	**total sq. ft.**

NOTE: 9 ft. main level walls

Upstairs, a computer loft overlooks the 2-story entry.

#50C ~8506

price code 24

dobson

When you order this plan you will receive a specification sheet for Integrity® Windows and Doors.

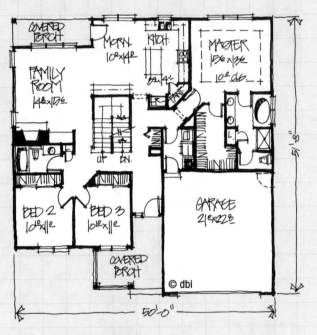

COVERED PORCH

MORN. 10⁰x14⁰

KITCH.

MASTER 15⁶x13⁶
10⁰ clg.

FAMILY ROOM 14⁸x17⁶

BED 2 10⁸x11⁰

BED 3 10⁸x11⁰

GARAGE 21⁶x22⁸

COVERED PORCH

© dbi

50'-0"

BED 5 12⁶x11¹⁰

COMP. NICHE

BED 4 11⁸x12⁶

1724   main floor
701   second floor
2425   total sq. ft.
NOTE: 9 ft. main level walls

Secondary bedrooms on the second level enjoy walk-in closets and access to a computer niche.

When you order this plan you will receive a specification sheet for Integrity® Windows and Doors.

#50C ~24011

price code 26

oliver

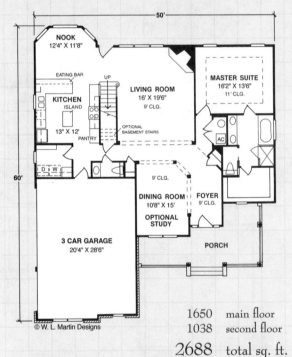

50'

NOOK 12'4" X 11'8"

EATING BAR

UP

LIVING ROOM 16' X 19'6" 9' CLG.

MASTER SUITE 16'2" X 13'6" 11' CLG.

KITCHEN ISLAND 13" X 12'

PANTRY

OPTIONAL BASEMENT STAIRS

AC

60'

9' CLG.

DINING ROOM 10'8" X 15'

FOYER 9' CLG.

OPTIONAL STUDY

3 CAR GARAGE 20'4" X 28'6"

PORCH

© W. L. Martin Designs

1650   main floor
1038   second floor
2688   total sq. ft.
NOTE: 9 ft. main level walls

WINDOW SEAT

SLOPE   SLOPE

PLAY ROOM 16' X 16'

ATTIC

AC

BEDROOM 4 12'6" X 11'4"

DN

BEDROOM 2 11'6" X 13'6"

BEDROOM 3 10'8" X 15'

SLOPE

This roomy play area could hold a computer, video games, or a pool table.

---

62   www.designbasics.com   a study of home ~ the outside in & the inside out

When you order this plan you will receive a specification sheet for Integrity® Windows and Doors.

#50C ~8100
price code 18

pebble creek

An unfinished area above the garage offers space for future expansion.

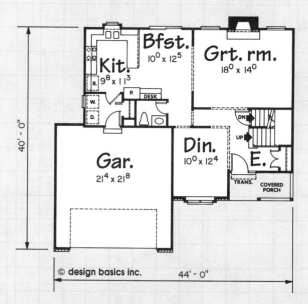

Bfst. 10⁰ x 12⁵

Grt. rm. 18⁰ x 14⁰

Kit. 9⁸ x 11³

R.

P. DESK

W.

D.

Gar. 21⁴ x 21⁸

Din. 10⁰ x 12⁴

DN

UP

E.

TRANS.

COVERED PORCH

40' - 0"

© design basics inc.   44' - 0"

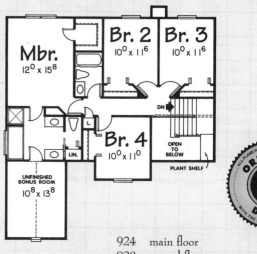

Mbr. 12⁰ x 15⁸

Br. 2 10⁰ x 11⁶

Br. 3 10⁰ x 11⁶

DN

Br. 4 10⁰ x 11⁰

LIN.

OPEN TO BELOW

UNFINISHED BONUS ROOM 10⁸ x 13⁸

PLANT SHELF

ORIGINAL DRAFT — ALL PLANS HAVE BEEN REGISTERED WITH THE U.S. COPYRIGHT OFFICE

924   main floor
920   second floor
1844 total sq. ft.

800-947-7526

#50C ~8503
price code 23

creedmore

When you order this plan you will receive a specification sheet for Integrity® Windows and Doors.

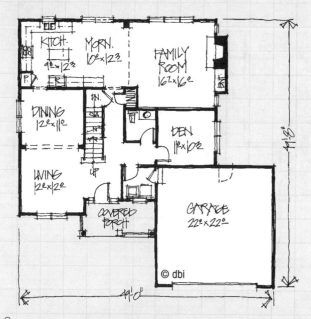

KITCH. 9⁸ x 12⁵

MORN. 10⁰ x 12³

FAMILY ROOM 16² x 16²

DINING 12² x 11⁰

DEN 11⁰ x 10²

LIVING 12² x 12²

UP

GARAGE 22⁰ x 22⁰

COVERED PORCH

41'-0"

49'-0"

© dbi

A spacious master suite and three secondary bedrooms make this home ideal for growing families.

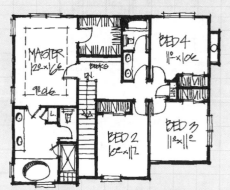

MASTER 12⁰ x 16⁶

9⁸ x 6⁶

BOOKS

BED 4 11⁰ x 10⁶

DN

BED 2 10² x 11²

BED 3 11² x 11²

L.

1251 main floor
1073 second floor
2324 total sq. ft.

NOTE: 9 ft. main level walls

63

#50C ~2281

price code 17

ingram

When you order this plan you will receive a specification sheet for Integrity® Windows and Doors.

#50C ~8095

price code 16

sun valley

When you order this plan you will receive a specification sheet for Integrity® Windows and Doors.

A triple-wide patio door provides a bright and sunny breakfast area.

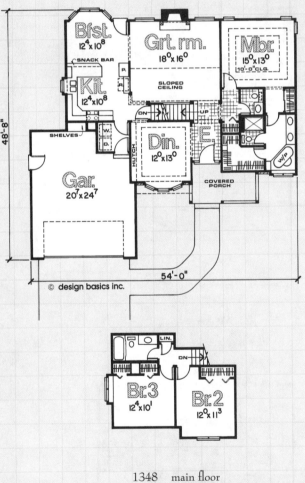

1348   main floor
430   second floor

1778   total sq. ft.

Unique ceilings add style in the dining room, the master bedroom and the great room.

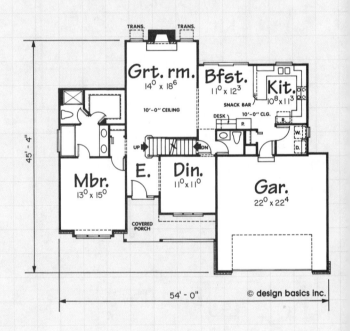

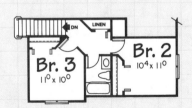

1298   main floor
396   second floor

1694   total sq. ft.

a study of home ~ the outside in & the inside out

When you order this plan you will receive a specification sheet for Integrity® Windows and Doors.

#50C ~24048
price code 13

cartwright

#50C ~8013
price code 13

gabriel bay

When you order this plan you will receive a specification sheet for Marvin® Windows and Doors.

Graceful columns define the living and dining rooms.

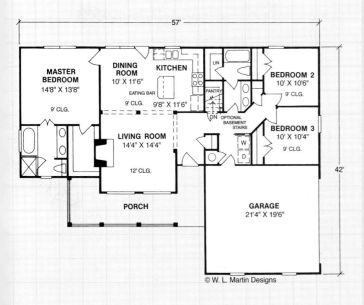

57'

MASTER BEDROOM
14'8" X 13'8"
9' CLG.

DINING ROOM
10' X 11'6"
EATING BAR
9' CLG.

KITCHEN
9'8" X 11'6"

LIN

PANTRY

BEDROOM 2
10' X 10'6"
9' CLG.

LIVING ROOM
14'4" X 14'4"
12' CLG.

DN OPTIONAL BASEMENT STAIRS

BEDROOM 3
10' X 10'4"
9' CLG.

W D

PORCH

GARAGE
21'4" X 19'6"

42'

© W. L. Martin Designs

1359 total sq. ft.

NOTE: 9 ft. main level walls

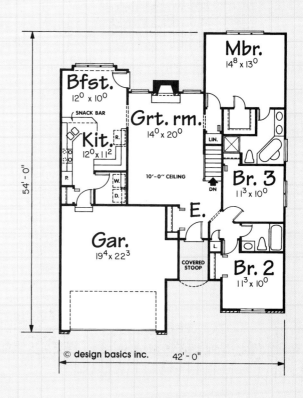

Bfst.
12⁰ x 10⁰
SNACK BAR

Kit.
12⁰ x 11²

Grt. rm.
14⁰ x 20⁰
10'-0" CEILING

Mbr.
14⁸ x 13⁰

LIN.

DN

Br. 3
11³ x 10⁰

Gar.
19⁴ x 22³

E.

COVERED STOOP

Br. 2
11³ x 10⁰

54' - 0"

© design basics inc.

42' - 0"

1392 total sq. ft.

this snack bar is ideal for interacting with the cook and grabbing quick meals.

design basics inc.
HOME PLAN DESIGN SERVICE

800-947-7526

65

bringing the Inside Out

These porches are shown for example purposes only
and are not from the bibury manor

front porches - character & charm

Nothing affects the character of a home like the look and feel of a front porch. Whether seen from the sidewalk, or enjoyed from within the coolness of its own shadows, a porch offers an air of nostalgic warmth – one that's symbolic of all that we've lost with time and everything we long for again.

For many of us, the porch conjures images of picturesque villages with tree-lined streets and picket-fenced lawns, where everyone knows one another's name. It's a place where we reach out and greet those passing by and extend a warm welcome to guests coming up the walk.

It's also a place we can escape to – a shelter within an open space that allows us to watch a thunderstorm within the storm itself.

Whatever a porch means to us, it stirs our senses from the inside out and transforms a house into a place called home.

www.designbasics.com

When you order this plan you will receive a specification
sheet for Marvin® Windows and Doors.

the bibury manor

#50C ~9172   price code 24

1280   main floor
1158   second floor

2438   total sq. ft.

NOTE: 9 ft. main level walls

MASTER
CLOSET
8' CH

MASTER
BATH
8' CH

OPEN TO
BELOW

MASTER
BEDROOM
13'-0" X 17'-0"
8'-11" CH

LEDGE

285 sq.ft.
OPTIONAL ATTIC
18'-0" X 13'-8"
8' CH

ATTIC
ACCESS

LADDER

DOWN

BALCONY
8' CH

CLO.

CLO CLO

BEDROOM 3
12'-4" X 11'-4"
10' CH

Optional Attic Space
Adds 285 Sq. Ft.

BEDROOM 2
13'-0" X 12'-0"
8' CH

BATH 2
8' CH

8' CH

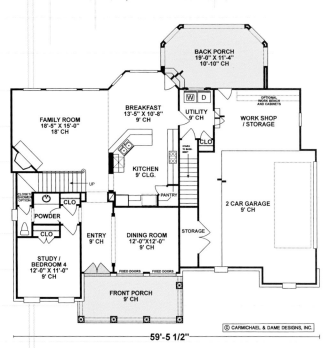

BACK PORCH
19'-0" X 11'-4"
10'-10" CH

FAMILY ROOM
18'-5" X 15'-0"
18' CH

BREAKFAST
13'-5" X 10'-8"
9' CH

W D

UTILITY
9' CH

OPTIONAL
WORK BENCH
AND CABINETS

WORK SHOP
/ STORAGE

KITCHEN
9' CLG.

STAIRS
TO BASE-
MENT

CLO

PANTRY

UP

CLOSET/
SHOWER
OPTION

CLO

2 CAR GARAGE
9' CH

POWDER

CLO

STORAGE

ENTRY
9' CH

DINING ROOM
12'-0" X 12'-0"
9' CH

STUDY /
BEDROOM 4
12'-0" X 11'-0"
9' CH

FIXED DOORS   FIXED DOORS

FRONT PORCH
9' CH

55'-11 1/2"

59'-5 1/2"

© CARMICHAEL & DAME DESIGNS, INC.

*On this elegant front porch
graceful arches frame three sets
of beautiful French doors.*

When you order this plan you will receive a specification
sheet for Marvin® Windows and Doors.

the ryland

#50C ~8519   price code 25

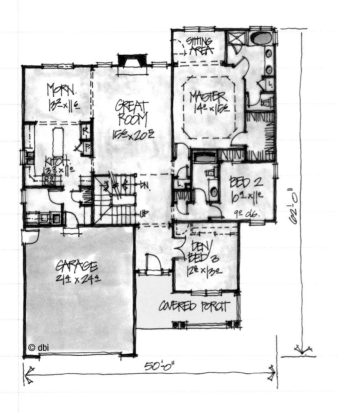

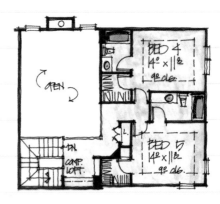

1902   main floor
691   second floor
2593   total sq. ft.
NOTE: 9 ft. main level walls

*A metal roof adds unique style
to this front porch.*

When you order this plan you will receive a specification sheet for Marvin® Windows and Doors.

the tealwood estate

#50C ~9162 price code 30

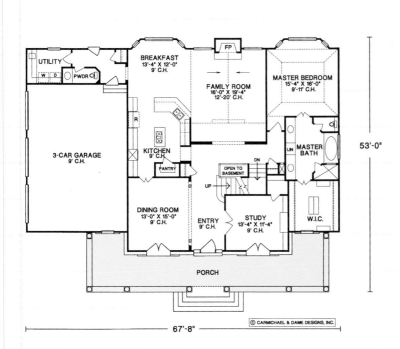

PORCH

67'-8"

© CARMICHAEL & DAME DESIGNS, INC.

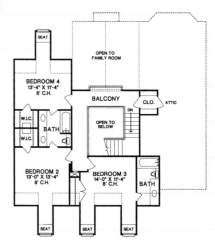

2116 main floor
956 second floor
3072 total sq. ft.

NOTE: 9 ft. main level walls

this picturesque porch creates mental pictures of neighbors stopping by to share a glass of cool lemonade.

design basics inc.
HOME PLAN DESIGN SERVICE

When you order this plan you will receive a specification sheet for Integrity® Windows and Doors.

the whitfield

#50C ~24138 price code 22

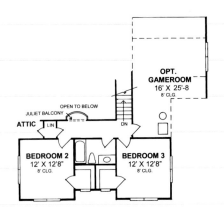

OPT. GAMEROOM
16' X 25'-8
8' CLG.

OPEN TO BELOW
JULIET BALCONY
ATTIC   LIN   DN

BEDROOM 2
12' X 12'8"
8' CLG.

BEDROOM 3
12' X 12'8"
8' CLG.

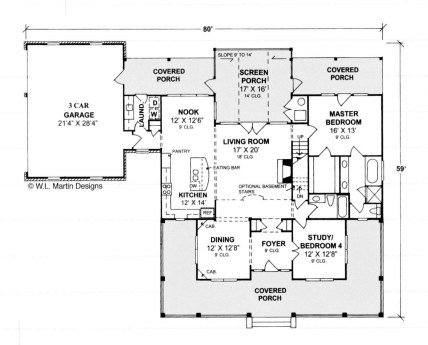

80'

COVERED PORCH

SLOPE 9' TO 14'

SCREEN PORCH
17' X 16'
14' CLG.

COVERED PORCH

3 CAR GARAGE
21'4" X 28'4"

LAUND.
D W

NOOK
12' X 12'6"
9' CLG.

LIVING ROOM
17' X 20'
18' CLG.

MASTER BEDROOM
16' X 13'
9' CLG.

PANTRY

EATING BAR

UP

59'

DW

KITCHEN
12' X 14'

REF

OPTIONAL BASEMENT STAIRS

DN

© W.L. Martin Designs

CAB.

DINING
12' X 12'8"
9' CLG.

FOYER
9' CLG.

STUDY/ BEDROOM 4
12' X 12'8"
9' CLG.

CAB.

COVERED PORCH

1736   main floor
516   second floor
2252   total sq. ft.
NOTE: 9 ft. main level walls

this large wrap-around porch extends a big welcome to guests.

a study of home ~ the outside in & the inside out

When you order this plan you will receive a specification
sheet for Marvin® Windows and Doors.

the anson

#50C ~5001 price code 16

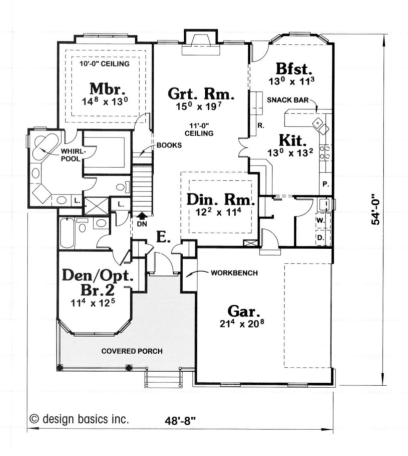

10'-0" CEILING

Mbr.
14⁸ x 13⁰

Grt. Rm.
15⁰ x 19⁷

11'-0"
CEILING

WHIRL-
POOL

BOOKS

Bfst.
13⁰ x 11³

SNACK BAR

R.

Kit.
13⁰ x 13²

L.

L.

DN

P.

Din. Rm.
12² x 11⁴

W.

D.

E.

WORKBENCH

**Den/Opt.
Br.2**
11⁴ x 12⁵

Gar.
21⁴ x 20⁸

COVERED PORCH

© design basics inc.

48'-8"

54'-0"

A deep front porch was
designed to accommodate a
lovely protruding bay window.

1653 total sq. ft.

NOTE: 9 ft. main level walls

design basics inc.
HOME PLAN DESIGN SERVICE

When you order this plan you will receive a specification
sheet for Marvin® Windows and Doors.

the timber crest

#50C ~9179 price code 28

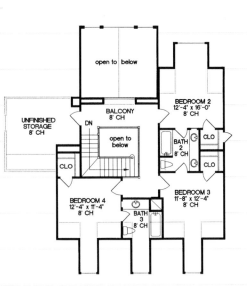

Unfinished Storage
Adds 171 Sq. Ft.

© CARMICHAEL & DAME DESIGNS, INC.

64'-8"

1907 main floor
908 second floor
2815 total sq. ft.
NOTE: 9 ft. main level walls

*A trio of dormers and a wide,
welcoming porch give this home
a country cottage charm.*

These porches are shown for example purposes only
and are not from the timber crest.

A front porch gives a
house a friendly character
that beckons us to stop
awhile, sit back, catch up
on neighborhood news and
renew ties with friends
and family.

the alanton

#50C ~24144 price code 23

On this front porch, a door to the laundry room provides quick access to the kitchen and half bath.

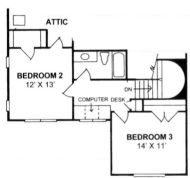

ATTIC

BEDROOM 2
12' X 13'

COMPUTER DESK

DN

BEDROOM 3
14' X 11'

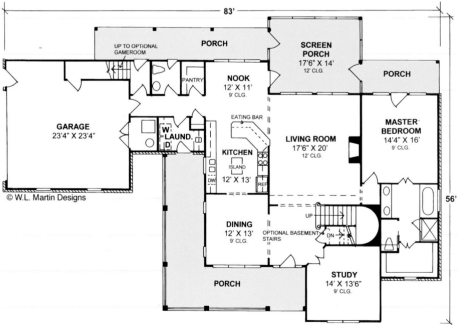

83'

UP TO OPTIONAL GAMEROOM

PORCH

SCREEN PORCH
17'6" X 14'
12' CLG.

PORCH

PANTRY

NOOK
12' X 11'
9' CLG.

GARAGE
23'4" X 23'4"

EATING BAR

W LAUND. D

LIVING ROOM
17'6" X 20'
12' CLG.

MASTER BEDROOM
14'4" X 16'
9' CLG.

KITCHEN
ISLAND
12' X 13'

DW

REF

© W.L. Martin Designs

DINING
12' X 13'
9' CLG.

OPTIONAL BASEMENT STAIRS

UP

DN

56'

STUDY
14' X 13'6"
9' CLG.

PORCH

Optional Gameroom
Adds 288 Sq. Ft.

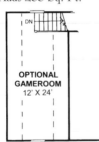

DN

OPTIONAL GAMEROOM
12' X 24'

2382 total sq. ft.

NOTE: 9 ft. main level walls

When you order this plan you will receive a specification
sheet for Integrity® Windows and Doors.

the fairmont

#50C ~5519   price code 24

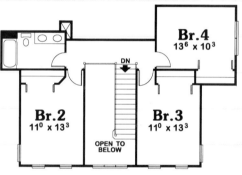

Br.4
13⁶ x 10³

DN

Br.2
11⁰ x 13³

OPEN TO
BELOW

Br.3
11⁰ x 13³

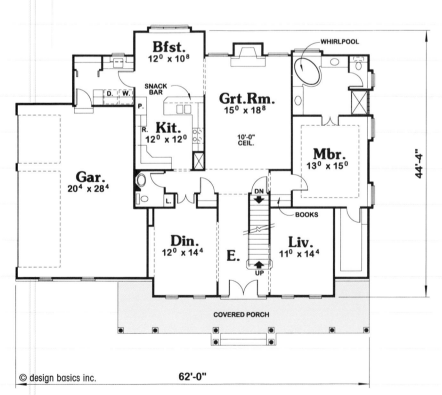

Bfst.
12⁰ x 10⁸

SNACK
BAR

WHIRLPOOL

Grt.Rm.
15⁰ x 18⁸

D. W.

P.

R.

Kit.
12⁰ x 12⁰

10'-0"
CEIL.

Mbr.
13⁰ x 15⁰

Gar.
20⁴ x 28⁴

L.

DN

BOOKS

44'-4"

Din.
12⁰ x 14⁴

E.

UP

Liv.
11⁰ x 14⁴

COVERED PORCH

© design basics inc.

62'-0"

1755 main floor
693   second floor
2448 total sq. ft.
NOTE: 9 ft. main level walls

*A decorative gable brings added
interest to this long porch.*

design basics inc
HOME PLAN DESIGN SERVICE
800-947-7526

When you order this plan you will receive a specification sheet for Integrity® Windows and Doors.

the roseland

#50C ~24139 price code 23

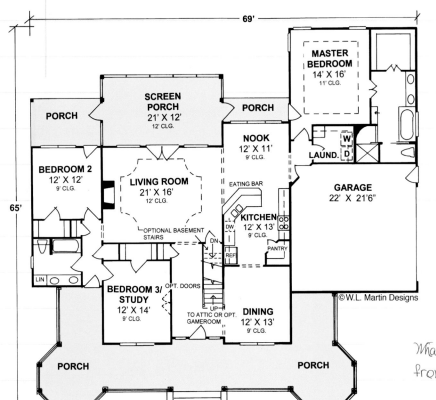

69'

65'

PORCH

SCREEN PORCH
21' X 12'
12' CLG.

PORCH

MASTER BEDROOM
14' X 16'
11' CLG.

BEDROOM 2
12' X 12'
9' CLG.

LIVING ROOM
21' X 16'
12' CLG.

NOOK
12' X 11'
9' CLG.

EATING BAR

W/D
LAUND.

GARAGE
22' X 21'6"

OPTIONAL BASEMENT STAIRS

KITCHEN
12' X 13'
9' CLG.

DW
REF
PANTRY

LIN

BEDROOM 3/ STUDY
12' X 14'
9' CLG.

OPT. DOORS

DN

UP
TO ATTIC OR OPT. GAMEROOM

DINING
12' X 13'
9' CLG.

© W.L. Martin Designs

PORCH

PORCH

Unfinished Storage
Adds 335 Sq. Ft.

DN

ATTIC / OPT. GAMEROOM
18' X 17'6"

BEDROOM 4
12' X 13'

2026   main floor
323   second floor
2349   total sq. ft.
NOTE: 9 ft. main level walls

What could be more charming than a front porch with a gazebo on each end?

www.designbasics.com   *a study of home ~ the outside in & the inside out*

the longworth estate

#50C ~9185 price code 22

In the front of the home, a wrap-
around veranda enjoys access to the
entry, dining room and breakfast area.

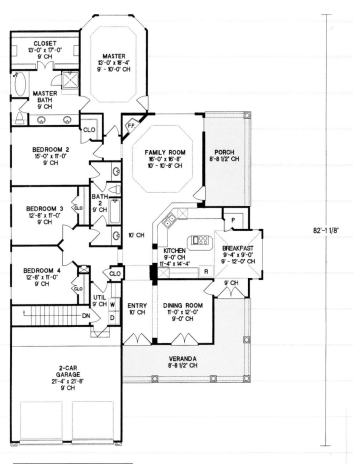

2211 total sq. ft.

NOTE: 9 ft. main level walls

© CARMICHAEL & DAME DESIGNS, INC.

HOME PLAN DESIGN SERVICE

When you order this plan you will receive a specification
sheet for Marvin® Windows and Doors.

the oakland

#50C ~24027   price code 21

*A gabled porch draws attention
to a lovely front entrance.*

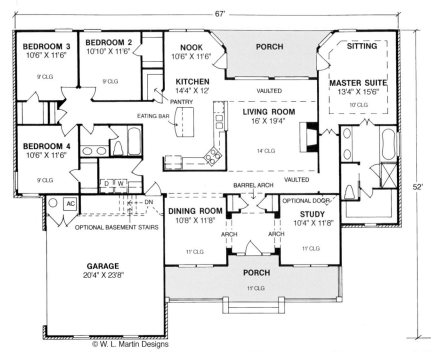

BEDROOM 3
10'6" X 11'6"
9' CLG

BEDROOM 2
10'10" X 11'6"
9' CLG

NOOK
10'6" X 11'6"

KITCHEN
14'4" X 12'

PANTRY

EATING BAR

BEDROOM 4
10'6" X 11'6"
9' CLG

PORCH

SITTING

MASTER SUITE
13'4" X 15'6"
10' CLG

VAULTED

LIVING ROOM
16' X 19'4"
14' CLG

VAULTED

D   W

AC

BARREL ARCH

OPTIONAL DOOR

OPTIONAL BASEMENT STAIRS

DN

DINING ROOM
10'8" X 11'8"
ARCH

STUDY
10'4" X 11'8"
ARCH

11' CLG

11' CLG

GARAGE
20'4" X 23'8"

PORCH
11' CLG

67'

52'

© W. L. Martin Designs

2144 total sq. ft.

NOTE: 9 ft. main level walls

a study of home ~ the outside in & the inside out

When you order this plan you will receive a specification
sheet for Marvin® Windows and Doors.

the westcott manor

#50C ~9171   price code 20

*Five stately columns and a metal roof
create a very distinctive porch.*

Optional Attic
Adds 627 Sq. Ft.

627 sq.ft.
OPTIONAL
ATTIC

DOWN

2040 total sq. ft.

NOTE: 9 ft. main level walls

9' CH

PORCH

BREAKFAST
11'-7" x 10'-0"
9' CH

BEDROOM 3
12'-0" x 11'-0"
9'-11" CH

BATH
3
CATH CLG

CLO

MASTER
BEDROOM
13'-0" x 15'-0"
9'-11" CH

FAMILY ROOM
17'-0" x 16'-0"
CATH CLG
9'-15' CH

CLO

UP
TO OPT
ATTIC

BEDROOM 2
12'-6" x 11'-0"
9' CH

MASTER
BATH
CATH CLG

KITCHEN
11'-7" x 14'-10"
9' CH

DOWN TO
BSMNT

GARAGE
21'-6" x 21'-8"
9' CH

PAN

BATH 2
9' CH

DINING ROOM
11'-0" x 12'-0"
9' CH

UTILITY

CLO

ENTRY
9' CH

W   D

COAT
CLO

MASTER CLOSET

CLO

CLO

PORCH
9' CH

STUDY /
BEDROOM 4
11'-2" x 11'-0"
9' CH

© CARMICHAEL & DAME DESIGNS, INC.

63'-6"

69'-5"

design basics inc
HOME PLAN DESIGN SERVICE   800-947-7526

back porches - privacy & comfort

Like front porches, back porches allow us to get away from our clocks and phones... calendars and computers...stacks of paper and lists of chores. But because they're secluded in the rear of the home, they're also more apt to be used as private retreats for those quiet times alone that feed the soul. Sipping coffee and reading the morning paper...planning your day, or the next twenty years...or just waiting for the fireflies to come out.

At other times, we share our back porches with others during neighborly cookouts and those comfortable conversations that last for hours among the closest of friends. Whether alone or surrounded by family and friends, these private porches have an almost magical quality - one that makes us less aware of the passing of time, while we make the most of the time we have.

When you order this plan you will receive a specification sheet for Marvin® Windows and Doors.

#50C ~24051

price code 15

the cabrie

Rear Elevation

This long wrap-around porch offers plenty of room for children to play on a rainy day.

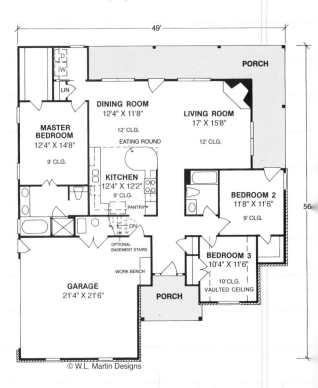

49'

56'

PORCH

DINING ROOM
12'4" X 11'8"
12' CLG.

LIVING ROOM
17' X 15'8"
12' CLG.

MASTER BEDROOM
12'4" X 14'8"
9' CLG.

EATING ROUND

KITCHEN
12'4" X 12'2"
9' CLG.

PANTRY

LIN

BEDROOM 2
11'8" X 11'6"
9' CLG.

OPTIONAL BASEMENT STAIRS

DN

BEDROOM 3
10'4" X 11'6"
10'CLG.
VAULTED CEILING

WORK BENCH

GARAGE
21'4" X 21'6"

PORCH

© W.L. Martin Designs

1541 total sq. ft.

NOTE: 9 ft. main level walls

www.designbasics.com

the creekbend manor

#50C ~9187 price code 17

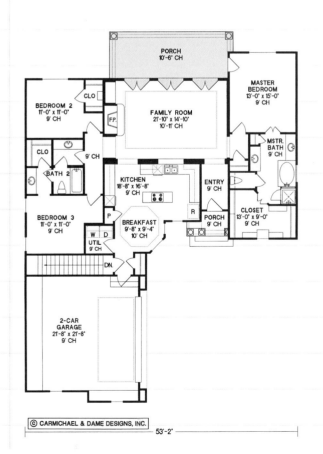

Rear Elevation

When you order this plan you will receive a specification sheet for Marvin® Windows and Doors.

1751 total sq. ft.

NOTE: 9 ft. main level walls

Three sets of french doors link the family room and this graceful porch - an ideal situation for larger gatherings.

© CARMICHAEL & DAME DESIGNS, INC.

the briar manor

#50C ~9207 price code 23

Rear Elevation

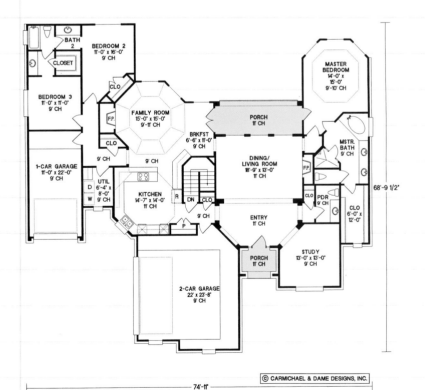

When you order this plan you will receive a specification
sheet for Marvin® Windows and Doors.

*this private porch is sure to
host many leisurely breakfasts
on quiet mornings.*

2331 total sq. ft.

NOTE: 9 ft. main level walls

a study of home ~ the outside in & the inside out

the windrush estate

#50C ~9198   price code 18

*this charming one-story's front and back
porches offer the best of both worlds.*

Rear Elevation

When you order this plan you will receive a specification
sheet for Marvin® Windows and Doors.

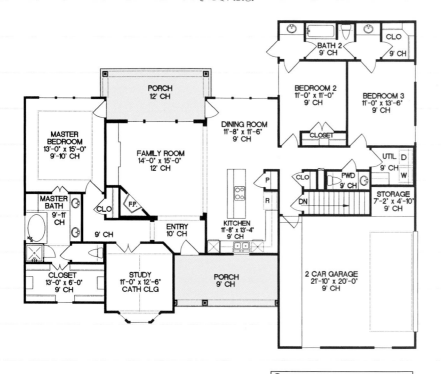

1876 total sq. ft.

NOTE: 9 ft. main level walls

52'-8"

65'-0"

© CARMICHAEL & DAME DESIGNS, INC.

the waterside estate

#50C ~9201   price code 19

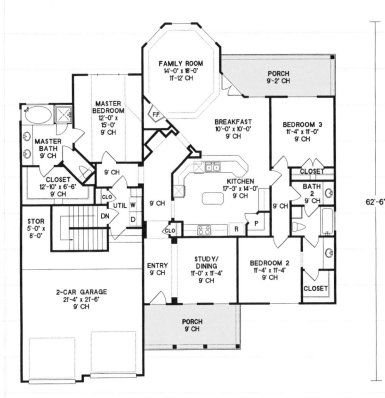

Rear Elevation

When you order this plan you will receive a specification sheet for Marvin® Windows and Doors.

62'-6"

1926 total sq. ft.

NOTE: 9 ft. main level walls

Guests in the family room and breakfast area are bound to flow onto this roomy back porch.

© CARMICHAEL & DAME DESIGNS, INC.

57'-0"

a study of home ~ the outside in & the inside out

the wellborn

#50C ~24153 price code 25

Rear Elevation

When you order this plan you will receive a specification sheet for Marvin® Windows and Doors.

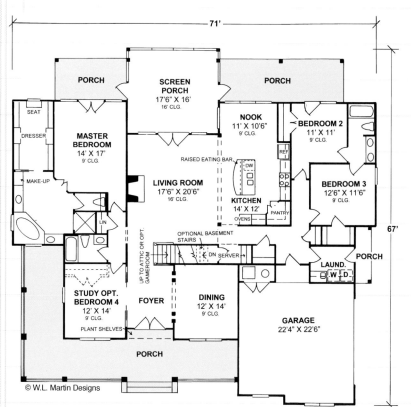

PORCH

SCREEN PORCH
17'6" X 16'
16' CLG.

PORCH

SEAT

DRESSER

MASTER BEDROOM
14' X 17'
9' CLG.

NOOK
11' X 10'6"
9' CLG.

BEDROOM 2
11' X 11'
9' CLG.

MAKE-UP

RAISED EATING BAR

REF

DW

LIVING ROOM
17'6" X 20'6"
16' CLG.

KITCHEN
14' X 12'

BEDROOM 3
12'6" X 11'6"
9' CLG.

LIN

OVENS

PANTRY

OPTIONAL BASEMENT STAIRS

UP TO ATTIC OR OPT. GAMEROOM

DN

SERVER

PORCH

STUDY OPT. BEDROOM 4
12' X 14'
9' CLG.

FOYER

DINING
12' X 14'
9' CLG.

LAUND.
W D

PLANT SHELVES

GARAGE
22'4" X 22'6"

PORCH

© W.L. Martin Designs

71'

67'

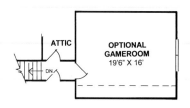

ATTIC

DN

OPTIONAL GAMEROOM
19'6" X 16'

Optional Game Room
Adds 312 Sq. Ft.

2512 total sq. ft.
NOTE: 9 ft. main level walls

With a huge wrap-around porch in the front and a 16-foot-high screened porch flanked by two open porches in the back, this home is a porch lover's dream.

design basics inc
HOME PLAN DESIGN SERVICE

When you order this plan you will receive a specification sheet for Marvin® Windows and Doors.

the whitmore

#50C ~9120   price code 33

Rear Elevation

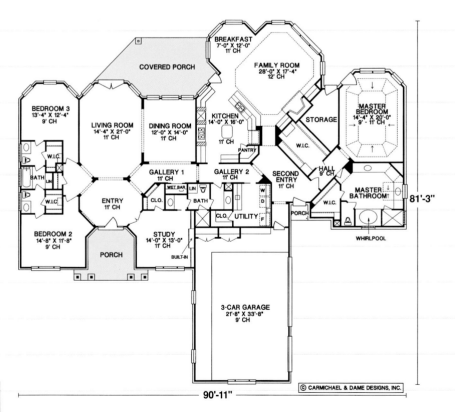

Optional Basement Access

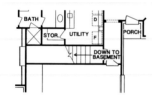

3312 total sq. ft.

NOTE: 9 ft. main level walls

Interesting angles give this garden porch lots of style.

© CARMICHAEL & DAME DESIGNS, INC.

Plenty of shade,
comfy furnishings
and cooling ceiling
fans make the
outdoors so
much nicer.

the stanton showcase

#50C ~9174   price code 26

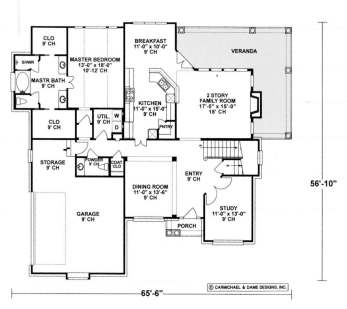

Rear Elevation

When you order this plan you will receive a specification sheet for Marvin® Windows and Doors.

Although wraparound verandas are customarily at the front of the home, this one at the back and side offers unusual privacy.

1844	main floor
794	second floor
2638	**total sq. ft.**

NOTE: 9 ft. main level walls

Option Attic Space
Adds 324 Sq. Ft.

When you order this plan you will receive a specification
sheet for Marvin® Windows and Doors.

the timberfield

#50C ~9211 price code 32

Rear Elevation

*Families who love the outdoors will
appreciate these stacked porches on the
main and second levels.*

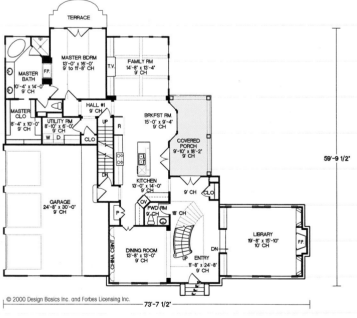

TERRACE

MASTER BDRM
13'-0" x 16'-0"
9' to 11'-8" CH

FAMILY RM
14'-8" x 13'-4"
9' CH

MASTER BATH
10'-4" x 14'-0"
9' CH

HALL #1
9' CH

BRKFST RM
15'-0" x 9'-4"
9' CH

MASTER CLO
8'-4" x 10'-0"
9' CH

UTILITY RM
8'-10" x 6'-0"
9' CH

COVERED PORCH
9'-10" x 18'-2"
9' CH

KITCHEN
13'-0" x 14'-0"
9' CH

GARAGE
24'-8" x 30'-0"
9' CH

PWD RM
9' CH

9' CH

CHINA CBNT

DINING ROOM
13'-8" x 13'-0"
9' CH

ENTRY
11'-4" x 24'-8"
9' CH

LIBRARY
19'-8" x 15'-10"
10' CH

© 2000 Design Basics Inc. and Forbes Licensing Inc.

73'-7 1/2"

59'-9 1/2"

Unfinished Storage
Adds 425 Sq. Ft.

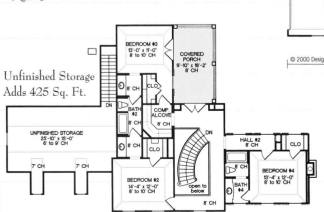

BEDROOM #3
13'-0" x 11'-0"
8' to 10' CH

COVERED PORCH
9'-10" x 18'-2"
8' CH

BATH #2
8' CH

COMP. ALCOVE
8' CH

UNFINISHED STORAGE
25'-10" x 15'-0"
6' to 9' CH

HALL #2
8' CH

7' CH   7' CH

BEDROOM #2
14'-4" x 12'-0"
8' to 10' CH

open to
below

BATH #4

BEDROOM #4
13'-4" x 12'-0"
8' to 10' CH

8' CH

2167	main floor
1092	second floor
3259	total sq. ft.

NOTE: 9 ft. main level walls

design basics inc.
HOME PLAN DESIGN SERVICE

When you order this plan you will receive a specification sheet for Marvin® Windows and Doors.

the balleroy

#50C ~9214 price code 33

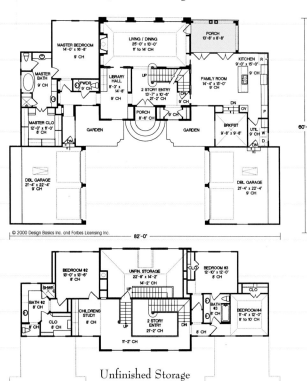

© 2000 Design Basics Inc. and Forbes Licensing Inc.

For added flexibility, this private back porch is accessed from the family room and the dining area.

2054	main floor
1281	second floor
3335	total sq. ft.

NOTE: 9 ft. main level walls

Unfinished Storage
Adds 583 Sq. Ft.

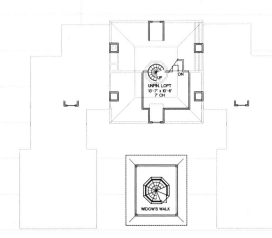

When you order this plan you will receive a specification
sheet for Marvin® Windows and Doors.

the greatwood showcase

#50C ~9183   price code 26

This back porch is accessed from the master
bedroom and the breakfast area.

Rear Elevation

1924   main floor
741   second floor

2665   total sq. ft.
NOTE: 9 ft. main level walls
Unfinished Storage
Adds 548 Sq. Ft.

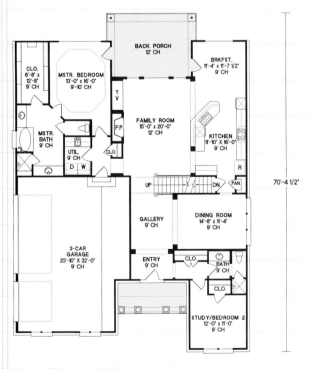

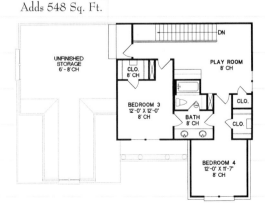

design basics inc.
HOME PLAN DESIGN SERVICE
800-947-7526

the baldwin court

#50C ~9176   price code 20

Just off the breakfast area, this roomy porch is sure to be a popular spot for summer dining.

When you order this plan you will receive a specification sheet for Marvin® Windows and Doors.

Rear Elevation

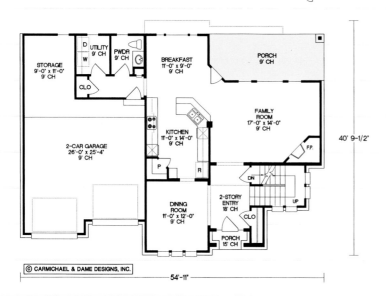

© CARMICHAEL & DAME DESIGNS, INC.

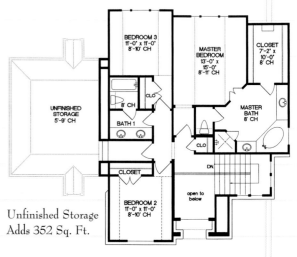

Unfinished Storage
Adds 352 Sq. Ft.

1063   main floor
979   second floor
2042   total sq. ft.

NOTE: 9 ft. main level walls

a study of home ~ the outside in & the inside out

the sherwood estate

When you order this plan you will receive a specification sheet for Marvin® Windows and Doors.

#50C ~9195   price code 19

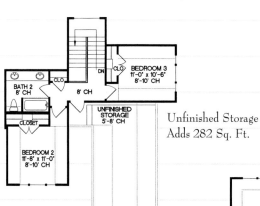

Unfinished Storage
Adds 282 Sq. Ft.

Rear Elevation

1446   main floor
456   second floor
1902   total sq. ft.

NOTE: 9 ft. main level walls

A porch just off the master bedroom
seems to invite stargazing.

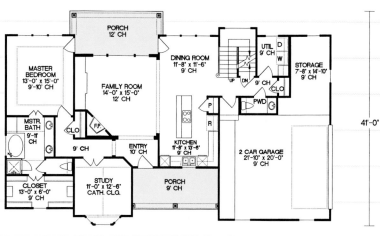

© CARMICHAEL & DAME DESIGNS, INC.

64'-4"

Free With Your
Homeplan Order!

With every set of plans ordered from this book, we will include a specification sheet calling out Marvin® or Integrity® windows and doors

design basics inc.
HOME PLAN DESIGN SERVICE

COPYRIGHT
Cans & Cannots

ALL DESIGN BASICS PLANS HAVE BEEN REGISTERED · ORIGINAL · DRAFT · WITH THE U.S. COPYRIGHT OFFICE

These days it seems almost everybody has a question about what can or cannot be done with copyrighted home plans. At Design Basics, we know U.S. copyright law can sometimes get complex and confusing, but here are a few of the basic points of the law you'll want to remember.

PROTECT YOUR RIGHTS

to build, modify and reproduce our home plans with a Design Basics construction license.

CONSTRUCTION LICENSE

Once you've purchased a plan from us and have received a Design Basics construction license

You Can ...

- Construct the plan as originally designed, or change it to meet your specific needs.
- Build it as many times as you wish *without* additional re-use fees.
- Make duplicate blueprint copies as needed for construction.

You Cannot ...

- Build our plans without a Design Basics construction license.
- Copy *any* part of our original designs to create another design of your own.
- Claim copyright on changes you make to our plans.
- Give a plan to someone else for construction purposes.
- Sell the plan.

The above points are provided as general guidelines only. Additional information is provided with each home plan purchase, or is available upon request at (800) 947-7526.

DESIGN BASICS' HOME PLAN LIBRARY

Impressions of Home™ Homes Designed with the Look You Want – 100 home plans from 1339' to 4139'. $4.95

Impressions of Home™ Homes Designed for the Way You Live – 100 home plans from 1191' to 4228'. $4.95

Impressions of Home™ Homes & Places for Real People – 100 home plans from 1341' to 4139'. $4.95

Study of Home™ - Special Places - 100 home plans from 1212' to 3914'. $4.95

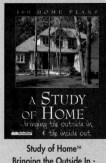

Study of Home™ How Home Has Changed - 100 home plans from 1212' to 4500'. $4.95

Study of Home™ Bringing the Outside In - 100 home plans from 1212' to 4500'. $4.95

Easy Living One-Story Designs™ 252 home plans from 962' to 3734'. $7.95

Gold Seal™ Home Plan Book Set - All 5 books for $50.00 or $10.00 each
Homes of Distinction - 86 plans under 1800'

Gold Seal™ Home Plan Book Set - All 5 books for $50.00 or $10.00 each
Homes of Sophistication - 106 plans, 1800'-2199'

Gold Seal™ Home Plan Book Set - All 5 books for $50.00 or $10.00 each
Homes of Elegance - 107 plans, 2200'-2599'

Gold Seal™ Home Plan Book Set - All 5 books for $50.00 or $10.00 each
Homes of Prominence - 75 plans, 2600'-2999'

Gold Seal™ Home Plan Book Set - All 5 books for $50.00 or $10.00 each
Homes of Grandeur - 68 plans, 3000'-4000'

Nostalgia Home Plans Collection™ A New Approach to Time-Honored Design - 70 home plans from 1339' to 3480'. $9.95

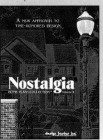

Nostalgia Home Plans Collection™ Vol. II - A New Approach to Time-Honored Design 70 home plans from 1191' to 3858'. $9.95

Timeless Legacy™, A Collection of Fine Home Designs by Carmichael & Dame – 52 home plans from 3300' to 4500'. $15.00

The Homes of Carmichael & Dame™ Vol. II 60 home plans from 1751' to 4228'. $9.95

W.L. Martin Home Designs™ 53 home plans from 1262' to 3914'. $9.95

The Narrow Home Plan™ Collection 258 home plans from 962' to 2517'. $14.95

Photographed Portraits of an American Home™ 100 home plans from 1205' to 4228'. $14.95

Reflections of an American Home™ Vol. III 50 home plans from 1341' to 3775'. $4.95

Seasons of Life™ Designs for Reaping the Rewards of Autumn - 100 home plans from 1212' to 3904'. $4.95

Seasons of Life™ Designs for Living Summer's Journey – 100 home plans from 1605' to 3775'. $4.95

Seasons of Life™ Designs for Spring's New Beginnings – 100 home plans from 1125' to 2537'. $4.95

Heartland Home Plans™ 120 home plans from 1212' to 2631'. $8.95

Gold Seal Favorites™ – 144 plans from the Gold Seal, Hometown, Multi-Family and Neighborhood in a Box Collections. 1125' to 5420'. $6.95

The Terra Cotta Collection™ 9 Southwestern Style Home Plans from 1528' to 2716'. $3.00

The Universal Collection™ 15 ADA Home Plans from 1394' to 2785'. $3.00

50CM

What's in a Design Basics Plan?

1. Cover Page. Each Design Basics home plan features the rendered elevation and informative reference sections including: general notes and design criteria;* abbreviations; and symbols for your Design Basics' plan.

2. Elevations. Drafted at ¼" scale for the front and ⅛" scale for the rear and sides. All elevations are detailed and an aerial view of the roof is provided, showing all framing members.

3. Foundations. Drafted at ¼" scale. Block foundations and basements are standard. We also show the HVAC equipment, structural information,* steel beam and pole locations and the direction and spacing of the floor system above.

4. Main Level Floor Plan. ¼" scale. Fully dimensioned from stud to stud for ease of framing. 2"x4" walls are standard. The detailed drawings include such things as structural header locations, framing layout and kitchen layout.

5. Second Level Floor Plan. ¼" scale. Dimensioned from stud to stud and drafted to the same degree of detail as the main level floor plan.*

6. Interior Elevations. Useful for the cabinet and bidding process, this page shows all kitchen and bathroom cabinets as well as any other cabinet elevations.

7. Electrical and Sections. Illustrated on a separate page for clarity, the electrical plan shows suggested electrical layout for the foundation, main and second level floor plans. Typical wall, cantilever, stair, brick and fireplace sections are provided to further explain construction of these areas.

Full Technical Support is available for any plan purchase from Design Basics. Our Technical Support Special provide unlimited technical support free of charge and answer questions regarding construction metho framing techniques and more. Please call 800-947-7526 for more information.

CONSTRUCTION LICENSE

When you purchase a Design Basics home plan, you receive a Construction License which gives you cert rights in building the home depicted in that plan, including:

No Re-Use Fee. As the original purchaser of a Design Basics home plan, the Construction Lice permits you to build the plan as many times as you like.

Local Modifications. The Construction License allows you to make modifications to your Design Bas plans. We offer a complete custom change service, or you may have the desired changes done locally a qualified draftsman, designer, architect or engineer.

Running Blueprints. Your plans are sent to you on vellum paper that reproduces well on your bluepr machine. The Construction License authorizes you or your blueprint facility, at your direction, to make many copies of the plan from the vellum masters as you need for construction purposes.

* Our plans are drafted to meet average conditions and codes in the state of Nebraska, at the time they are designed. Because co and requirements can change and may vary from jurisdiction to jurisdiction, Design Basics Inc. cannot warrant compliance with specific code or regulation. All Design Basics plans can be adapted to your local building codes and requirements. It is the responsibl of the purchaser and/or builder of each plan to see that the structure is built in strict compliance with all governing municipal co (city, county, state and federal).

TO ORDER DIRECT: CALL 800-947-7526
MONDAY – FRIDAY 7:00 a.m. – 6:00 p.m. CST

Name _____

Company _____

Street _____

_____
(Packages cannot be shipped to a P.O. Box.)

Above Address: ☐ business address ☐ residential address

City _____ State _____ Zip _____

Phone ( ) _____ FAX ( ) _____

e-mail _____

☐ VISA [VISA]   ☐ MasterCard [MasterCard]   Credit Card: ☐☐☐☐☐☐☐☐☐☐☐☐☐☐☐☐
We appreciate it when you use VISA or MasterCard.

☐ Check enclosed ☐ AMEX ☐ Discover

Signature _____

Expiration Date: ☐☐ / ☐☐

✔	HOME PLAN PRODUCTS	PLAN #	QTY.	PRICE	SHIPPING & HANDLING	TOTAL
☐	1 Set of Master Vellums or 5 Sets of Blueprints					$
☐	Add'l. Sets of Blueprints - $20.00 Carmichael & Dame Plans – $40.00					$
☐	Materials & Estimator's Workbook - $50.00 (If Available)					$
☐	Study Print & Furniture Layout Guide™ - $50.00					$
☐	Complete Plan Book Library – $150.00					$
☐						$
☐						$
BOOK NUMBER	BOOK NAME					$
						$

• CALL FOR • Shipping & Handling Charges

CALL 800-947-7526
OR MAIL ORDER TO: Design Basics
11112 John Galt Blvd.
Omaha, NE 68137
fax: (402) 331-5507
www.designbasics.com

• No COD Orders • US Funds Only •
NO REFUNDS OR EXCHANGES, PLEASE

Subtotal $

TX Res. Add 6.25% Tax (Carmichael & Dame Plans Only)
NE Residents Add 6.5% Sales Tax $

design basics inc. HOME PLAN DESIGN SERVICE PRICES SUBJECT TO CHANGE

Total $

PLAN PRICE SCHEDULE

PLAN CODE	TOTAL SQ. FT.	PRICE
9	900' - 999'	$525
10	1000' - 1099'	$535
11	1100' - 1199'	$545
12	1200' - 1299'	$555
13	1300' - 1399'	$565
14	1400' - 1499'	$575
15	1500' - 1599'	$585
16	1600' - 1699'	$595
17	1700' - 1799'	$605
18	1800' - 1899'	$615
19	1900' - 1999'	$625
20	2000' - 2099'	$635
21	2100' - 2199'	$645
22	2200' - 2299'	$655
23	2300' - 2399'	$665
24	2400' - 2499'	$675
25	2500' - 2599'	$685
26	2600' - 2699'	$695
27	2700' - 2799'	$705
28	2800' - 2899'	$715
29	2900' - 2999'	$725
30	3000' - 3099'	$735
31	3100' - 3199'	$745
32	3200' - 3299'	$755
33	3300' - 3399'	$765
34	3400' - 3499'	$775
35	3500' - 3599'	$785
36	3600' - 3699'	$795
37	3700' - 3799'	$805
38	3800' - 3899'	$815
39	3900' - 3999'	$825
40	4000' - 4099'	$835
41	4100' - 4199'	$845
42	4200' - 4299'	$855
43	4300' - 4399'	$865
44	4400' - 4499'	$875
45	4500' - 4599'	$885
46	4600' - 4699'	$895
47	4700' - 4799'	$905
48	4800' - 4899'	$915
49	4900' - 4999'	$925
2X	Duplex	$795
3X	Tri-Plex	$895
4X	4-Plex	$995

PRICES SUBJECT TO CHANGE